Miss Kathleen Goligher

Through whose wonderful physical mediumship the experiments described in this book were rendered possible.

KATHLEEN GOLIGHER
Physical Medium

Previously Published as

THE REALITY OF PSYCHIC PHENOMENA

RAPS, LEVITATIONS, ETC.

BY

W. J. CRAWFORD, D. Sc.

Lecturer in mechanical engineering, the municipal technical institute, Belfast; extramural lecturer in mechanical engineering, queen's university of Belfast; author of "elementary graphic statics." "calculations on the entropy-temperature chart," etc.

First Edition 1916
This Edition 2008

Printed and bound by CPI Antony Rowe, Eastbourne

Published by
SDU PUBLICATIONS
www.sdu3.com
ISBN 9781905961108

PREFACE

The experiments described were carried out during portions of the years 1915 and 1916, many of them being recorded in the pages of Light at the time. I have endeavoured in this work to put them more or less in logical sequence so that the reader may understand the processes that led me to enunciate the cantilever theory. Much of the text is, however, now published for the first time. I am indebted to Mr. Seamus Stoupe of the Art Department of the technical institute, Belfast, for the two photographs of apparatus; and I have to express my thanks to Messrs W. & T. Avery, Ltd., for the use of their weighing and measuring machines.

I do not discus in this book the question of the identity of the invisible operators. That is left for another occasion. But, in order that there may be no misapprehension, I wish to state explicitly that I am personally satisfied they are the spirits of human beings who have passed into the Beyond.

W. J. Crawford.
Belfast, Sept. 1916.

CONTENTS

Chapter		Page
I	Preliminary remarks on the composition of the circle, the phenomena, etc.	1
II	Phonograph record of the noises	20
III	Reaction during levitation of the table	25
IV	Some miscellaneous experiments, observations and calculations	44
V	Conditions above, under, and round the levitated table	58
VI	Levitation directly above the platform of a weighing machine	70
VII	Experiments with compression spring balance underneath the levitated table	79
VIII	Completion of the experiments on levitation	102
IX	A cantilever theory for levitation	111
X	Raps	133
XI	The rod theory for raps	142
XII	Miscellaneous experiments	155
XIII	General conclusions	163

THE REALITY OF PSYCHIC PHENOMENA

CHAPTER I

PRELIMINARY REMARKS ON THE COMPOSITION OF THE CIRCLE, THE PHENOMENA, ETC.

The Circle with whose voluntary co-operation I have carried out the experiments recorded in this book, consists of seven members, as follows:— Mr. Morrison, Mrs. Morrison, Miss Kathleen Goligher, Miss Lily Goligher, Miss Anna Goligher, Mr. Goligher and Master Samuel Goligher. It is altogether a family affair, being composed of father, four daughters, son, and son-in-law, for Mrs Morrison is the sister of the medium. All the members are mediums in a greater or less degree, the various phases of the phenomena presented consisting of trance speaking, automatic writing, table movements, and so on. One member of the family, Miss Kathleen Goligher, the youngest of the four daughters, is, however, a medium of outstanding merit. This young lady was born on June 27, 1898. She has probably inherited her mediumistic tendencies, for there are psychic traditions in the family on the mother's side. Her mediumship was discovered, as so often happens, more or less by accident. Some three years ago the family was desirous of sitting for physical phenomena, and formed in the ordinary way, a circle. Rappings were obtained almost at once, and then by a process of elimination—in which the medium was eliminated amongst others—her gift was discovered. Since then the family has regularly conducted its development, week by week, with the result that the physical phenomena now presented are powerful and well regulated.

The whole of the family look upon Spiritualism as their religion. They attend no church other than the spiritualistic, but they are devoted in their attachment to that—several of the young ladies being members of the choir or serving in other capacities, while Mr. Morrison is a member of the Committee, and works hard in the interests of the Society. They are simple and harmonious in their home life, and are in every way fit recipients of the extraordinary phenomena obtained through their instrumentality.

The séances for my experimental work were mostly held in an attic in the house occupied by the medium's family, though I have occasionally held them in my own house, and I have also witnessed the phenomena in the houses of friends. The room or house where the séances are held seems to make little or no difference, for a few minutes after the circle is formed, wherever it be, phenomena begin to be produced. The attic above referred to was, however, most suitable, as it is kept for no other purpose than for use as a séance-room, and the family also find it more convenient to assemble in their own house. For it must be remembered that each one of my experimental sittings necessitated the attendance and co-operation of eight persons, and in addition there was a great deal of preliminary work to be attended to, such as the provision of apparatus, etc. For psychical research is like no other kind of research. Before we can expect anything worth having in the way of results we must have the following set of conditions as nearly perfect as possible:—

(a) A very powerful medium.

(b) A circle of sitters supporting the medium.

(c) The medium and sitters to be imbued with the seriousness and wonder of the phenomena presented—to be linked together, as it were, by the one object of getting the most out of the phenomena for the common good.

(d) A band of operators who have the same objects in view as those mentioned in (c). Mischievous operators or others who will not or cannot co-operate with the experimenter are useless.

(e) The phenomena must not be produced spontaneously, but must be under command.

I need hardly say that if money be the chief and only object of the medium's ambition, practically no experimental work can be done. It is a matter of experience—my experience, anyway—that the medium and sitters must not develop any form of material greed, or the phenomena become undependable and unreliable. This does not mean, of course, that a medium may not take reasonable remuneration; but it decidedly means that if she is purely and absolutely concerned with the amount of money she can make out of her psychic gifts, her phenomena suffer.

The five conditions given above for successful experimental work in the psychic realm are, in my opinion, absolutely essential. Omit any one of them, and the results suffer from a scientific point of view. This is probably the reason why so little such work is done. The required conditions are generally too much for the experimenter.

Unless the invisible operators co-operate heartily in experimental work, the results are likely to be of small value, for it goes without saying that the spontaneous phenomena are of little use. I think that the thing which has chiefly struck me, during the course of my investigation, has been the wonderful co-operation between the operators and myself. One scarcely becomes used, no matter how long one works at psychical phenomena, to having one's behest's attended to by beings who are entirely beyond the confines of bodily sight. But I can say truly that during all my experimental séances every demand I made of the operators was either successfully carried out or was attempted. They were evidently anxious to submit to every scientific test imposed. Sometimes, but very occasionally, when something stood in the way of the accomplishment of some of my requests, they would spell out a word or sentence which would enable me to understand the obstruction in the way of the production of the phenomenon I particularly wanted. Sometimes I have reason to suppose they would, of their own volition, bring to my attention phases of an experiment which I had overlooked. In the whole of the five conditions enumerated above I have been fortunate in obtaining a very high degree of perfection. Indeed, I cannot see how they could have been greatly improved upon.

I have said that most of my experimental séances were held in an attic in the house occupied by the medium's family. The floor of the room is bare. Each member of the circle possesses a special wooden chair and sits on no other (Except on special occasions when I altered the arrangement). Besides the chairs the only other furniture in the room consists of the séance table and a few ornaments on the mantelpiece (except of course when I brought in apparatus). [During the last experimental sitting, however, there was a small cabinet in a corner of the room, the circle having commenced to sit for materialisations; but during all the other séances the room was as I have described.]

For the general purpose of lighting the séance chamber, a gas jet enclosed in a lantern having a red glass sliding front and side is used. The intensity of the light can thus be considerably varied by means of an ordinary cock. When one becomes used to the red light, the visibility becomes quite good—most objects in the room are quite plainly seen. It is to be regretted that psychical phenomena cannot as a rule be produced in full white light; but we have to take this matter as we find it and submit to the conditions imposed by nature.

For reading small numbers and graduations, such as those on the steelyard of a weighing machine, I most often employed an electric pocket-lamp with the lens covered with a piece of red tissue-paper.

The séance is opened with the singing of a hymn and a prayer. In a few minutes light raps are usually heard near the medium, which quickly increase in intensity. Within a quarter of an hour most of the phenomena are often in full swing. A hymn is sung occasionally during the course of the séance. The sitting is closed by prayer.

The method of conducting the circle is as simple as possible. The members simply sit round in approximately circle formation and clasp each other's hands in chain order. The séance table is placed on the floor within the circle. I have found by experience that for the first thirty minutes or so of the sitting, quickest and best results are obtained if the chain formation of hands is adhered to; after that it matters very little whether the circle clasp hands or whether they put hands on knees. This points to the likelihood that during the commencement of a séance processes are in operation which are more or less in abeyance later on, when a condition of psychic equilibrium has been established. I will describe an experiment which would appear to verify this, where the medium was seated on a weighing-machine near the commencement of the séance.

The phenomena presented are purely physical, and physical in the sense that the results depend upon the action of psychic force upon material bodies. No materialisations or partial materialisations have so far occurred. Therefore such phenomena, being due to the action of psychic force alone, can be studied in a more satisfactory manner than would be the case if they were complicated by more advanced types. I hold strongly to the opinion that if the processes resulting in the application of psychic force are once really discovered, then the rest of psychic phenomena will rapidly fall into place and be understandable. Psychic energy—as evidenced in good physical séances—is at the root of the whole thing, and it is useless to expect any great advance until its laws have been unravelled. The Goligher circle allows of the display of psychic force to the very best advantage. Not only is the force exerted of large magnitude, but it is also accurate, under command, and infinitely variable. Further, all the movements of matter produced by it are telekinetic, or produced without material contact. This is to be thoroughly understood. *In no experiment which I describe in this book was there any contact between any portion of the body or dress of the medium or sitters and the material body under psychic action.*

I would, speaking broadly, divide the phenomena produced into two classes: (1) impacts, and (2) movements of material bodies against the action of forces such as those of friction and gravity. The impact phenomena consist of raps and their variations, and are not caused by the action of matter on matter; for instance, I would not term the action of a table leg being raised and being struck on the floor (which I have often observed) an impact phenomenon. The impact type is that where a blow is caused by psychic force being applied suddenly to a material body.

Examples of this type are many at the Goligher circle; amongst others the following variations commonly occur:— (a) raps of all degrees of loudness from the slightest taps to blows which might verily be produced by a sledge-hammer; (b) combinations of raps, such as single knocks, double knocks, treble knocks (two fast, one slow), volleys of raps, imitations of tunes and dances (the latter including the sand-dance, from the kind of shuffling produced)—in fact, every kind and combination of rap it is possible to imagine; (c) specialities, such as the imitation of a bouncing ball (most perfect in sound quality), imitation of a match being struck, imitation of a man walking and a horse trotting, imitation of the leg of the table being sawn, of the floor being rubbed with sandpaper, and so on.

To the second class belong all movements of material bodies due to the action of psychic force upon them. The levitation of a table is the most spectacular and common, but there are also all kinds of motions of the table upon the floor—translational, rotational, and combinations of these two. The table is sometimes gently lowered about two legs to the floor and replaced in position. A metal trumpet is waved about in the air. A small hand-bell is taken up and rung. The sitters are sometimes psychically "touched."

A great many people have now seen the phenomena produced through the circle, and I have yet to meet the person who was not deeply impressed. The unseen operators seem to enjoy convincing the believer and sceptic alike of the reality of psychic force. In this connection the reader will be interested to hear how they treat the ordinary lay visitor. The visitor is usually invited to enter the circle, to lay hold of the table (at the moment stationary) and to endeavour to prevent it from moving. Then the tussle begins. If he is very muscular and has his weight nicely placed over the centre of the table, the experimenter may have the better of matters for short time, though it is amusing to the onlookers to see how hard he is pressed. But sooner or later (usually sooner) the table eludes him, jumps this way and that about the floor, tilts, twists, and, if his muscular pressure is momentarily relaxed, levitates. Then there is more trouble. The table, once levitated, strongly objects to be pushed to the floor, and few persons can push it there, no matter how they try. Then after a struggle with the levitating force the table becomes tranquil on the floor and the visitor is invited to sit on it. But he does not sit long. In a moment or two it gently rises on two legs and slides him off. Finally it escorts him outside the circle, the "escorting" consists of forcible ejection by an overwhelming pressure against his body.

Fraud

Of course, all experiments recorded in this book depend for any value they may have on the fact that the table movements, levitations, raps, blows, and other phenomena are genuine productions due to the action of psychic force and are in no way caused by fraudulent action on the part of the medium or members of the circle; and by fraudulent action I refer not only to conscious but also to unconscious imposture, for without doubt there are cases in which a medium, quite unconsciously to herself, uses methods for the production of phenomena that amount to fraud.

I propose to give here briefly a few of the facts which show that the phenomena produced at the Goligher circle are the genuine thing and are in no way due to conscious or unconscious action on the part of the medium or sitters.

(1) The medium and her family are upright, religious-minded people, who keep to a high moral standard in their daily lives. Each and every one of them is incapable of any wrong action with regard to the ordinary affairs of life. They all look upon the phenomena as specially presented to show that life is continuous after bodily death, of which they are all now absolutely certain; in other words, they are all convinced Spiritualists, and I could not imagine anything that could alter their convictions in this matter.

(2) All séances are looked upon as religious institutions. They are invariably opened and closed by prayer. No levity is permitted.

(3) All members of the circle are my personal friends, and I have had an intimate knowledge of them for three years. I understand exactly their views of life and of things in general, their idiosyncrasies, their high standard of rectitude, and their attitude regarding the phenomena and its relation to themselves.

(4) The medium is the least enthusiastic member of the circle. She is the only one who cares little about the phenomena. I think she sits more as an obligation to the others than for any innate satisfaction to herself. Whether phenomena are obtained at the séances or not does not affect her in the least.

(5) The medium is a private one. She charges nothing. I have never paid her one penny for any of the séances she has so kindly given me. She is very averse to looking upon her mediumship as a commercial asset.

(6) No dark séances are held. The light is usually strong enough—after the eyes get accustomed to its red colour—to see quite plainly all the sitters. It is a subdued kind of light, issuing from a large surface of ordinary gas flame. The only difficulty in the visibility is where a table or other large body casts a shadow over a portion of the floor. The hands of the sitters can nearly always be quite plainly seen, and it is a simple experiment, while the séance table is levitated a foot or more in the air, to ask the sitters to raise their hands (joined in chain order) up to the level of their heads, so that the observer can be quite sure that the hands have nothing whatever to do with the phenomenon. The observer at this time may be *within the circle*, and he may move anywhere inside it so long as he does not get immediately in front of the medium. The only place in shadow, if the table is comparatively large (if it is a small one he can see right round it), is between the foot of the table and the medium. But even with the largest table it is sometimes possible to see completely under it (as I have done), to see the feet and bodies of all present at rest and hands held together in chain order, while the table has been steadily levitated. It comes to this, then, that the only region not always visible (and this is only sometimes the case) is the region in the neighbourhood of the medium just above and on the floor. In many cases of levitation, the levitated table, the space all round, above, and over it, and all the sitters are quite plainly visible.

(7) The medium was quite conscious during all my experimental investigations, and any fraud presented would therefore be in the nature of deliberate action. She herself was always keenly interested in the experiments, and has told me she enjoys such sittings much more that ordinary

development séances. It was amusing to watch how interested she was when, say, an electric bell was rung by the reaction under a levitated table, or when other experimental work was in progress. Many times I have observed the keenness with which she followed what went on, evidently forgetting for the time being that she herself was the prime cause of all the phenomena, and that without her there would have been nothing.

(8) It matters not one whit whether the members of the circle come to the séance-room in their ordinary boots or shoes, in their stocking soles or in soft felt slippers. The thunderous blows on the floor within the circle are not in the least affected as regards magnitude. One distinguished visitor to the circle, after hearing the tremendous din caused by the "raps," had the fact pointed out to him that all the members wore soft felt slippers, and that with hands all visibly joined it was an impossibility to produce such noises normally. The medium on this occasion was asked to remove her slippers in order that it might be shown no hard substance was concealed therein; which, of course, she immediately did, with results evidently satisfactory to the visitor.

(9) A great many people have been invited to visit the circle and witness the phenomena. I think I can say that not one of all these has come away from it without the assurance that "there is something in psychic force," be he previously sceptic, believer, or a sitter "on the fence." Of course, the visitor is not always certain that the phenomena are produced by spirits of the dead; but at least he is sure of this, that they are genuine and in no way due to normal action on the part of the medium or members of the circle.

(10) The magnitude of the motions applied to the table must be seen to be believed. Often a force approximating a hundredweight is exerted. A visitor is invited to enter the circle, as already explained, to lay hold of the table, and to try to prevent its motion. I have never yet seen this

successfully accomplished. Now, the only way such movements could be given normally to the table is by the feet of the medium, for all hands and bodies of sitters and medium are quite plainly seen, and the only part that may be in shadow is near the feet of the medium. It can be proved conclusively by direct experiment that even if the medium were to lie back in her chair, spread her feet out so that they were under the surface of the table, eighteen inches or more away, and endeavour to levitate it or move it about, such motion of her body would be immediately detected, and that a man pressing immediately over the table could prevent even the slightest motion by a ridiculously small effort, whereas, as already mentioned, the strongest man cannot in reality do so. The leverage from the medium's feet to her body is so great that a very small force only is required to prevent motion.

(11) If the medium leans back in her chair and endeavours to levitate the table with her feet, she may do so for a few seconds, in a stilted jerky kind of fashion; but the real levitation is quite different in character and quality from the spurious one, and the latter can only be maintained for a very short time.

(12) I have spent many hours within the circle in all places round it, and I have continually worked under the levitated table and between the levitated table and the medium; I have had complicated instruments below the table; I have often placed by arm and hand in the space between medium and table and felt her feet and legs absolutely still during the course of experiments in which the table was levitated and the instruments were registering below it; and I say finally that if the medium had desired to impose, she could not, no matter how she tried, have kept the table levitated and the instruments registering at the same time, while my hands were on such instruments and I myself close to her feet and working between her and the table.

(13) It is well to analyse a few of the experimental results with regard to the theory of fraud. The experiments in Chapter III Show conclusively that while the table is steadily levitated nearly the whole of its weight is upon the medium. Therefore it follows that if anyone is lifting the table with any part of his body, it is the medium, and the others are not concerned. The medium's hands are always quite visible, and the only part of her sometimes in deep shadow (if the table is a comparatively large one) is from her knees downwards. Now, it is impossible for her to put her feet below the surface of the table unless she leans back in her chair and sprawls her body forward into the circle space (as already mentioned), and such a manœuvre would be instantly detected. But if we suppose (taking the most unfavourable case) that she could do this, the only way she could levitate the table would be with her feet. We therefore narrow down any theory of fraud to the surreptitious use by the medium of her feet.

Consider experiment 50, where there was a large compression balance below the table during levitation. The balance was reading 30 lbs. while the table was in the air a foot above the floor. How could this be accomplished by fraudulent means on the part of the medium? Only in one way. One foot would have to be levitating the table and the other would have to be pressing down on the pan of the balance, an exceedingly difficult matter indeed, and practically impossible, as experiment proves, even when all possible help is given to the medium, including holding her arms tight to prevent her falling. Supposing, however, that she could accomplish this, how is it that for the same table and the same balance, the balance read the same amount within half a pound every time I tried the experiment, and I tried it often? How could she gauge the downward force so accurately each time? Would there not be a variation of several pounds at least?

Experiment further shows that the downward force on the balance is applied gradually and at a uniform rate, and that the table always springs into the air at the same instant, i.e. when the balance reads just above 30 lbs., and that there is never any variation during successful levitation in this arrangement. If the medium pressed down on the balance with one foot, would she be able to apply the pressure so gradually and uniformly, and would she be able to levitate the table always at the same relative instant?

In Experiment 46 (E) I actually placed my hand and part of my arm in the scale-pan of the balance while it was registering and while the table was levitated above it. *There was nothing in the pan*, and furthermore both the levitation and the reading on the balance were in this instance unaffected.

Take Experiments 48 and 49. The medium's feet were near the nail N on the floor. I placed them there and felt them from time to time, and *they never moved*. There were *three* sets of phenomena in simultaneous operation in these experiments: (1) table levitated; (2) balance B reading; (3) balance S reading. My position was near S, and my hands were continually moving to and fro in front of the medium's feet and between her feet and the table. Furthermore, during half a dozen readings or more I took, the readings on the balances hardly varied at all.

Take Experiments 51 and 52. Those show conclusively that when the table is levitated above the platform E, there is no reaction on the platform until it reaches a height of about three inches above the floor. That is to say, if the medium is fraudulent, she lifts the table with one foot only, until E is about three inches above the floor, and *then* (and not until then) places the other foot on E and (as the tabulation of Experiment 52 shows) increases with that foot the pressure on the platform as the latter is gradually raised in height. This would be a silly procedure, as (if the thing were possible at all, which it is not) she would naturally press on the platform at its lowest position, and would not wait until it was about three inches above the floor and then nicely regulate her pressure to about three-quarters of a pound.

In Experiment 22 it is shown that the table may have its weight so greatly increased that a strong man leaning over it cannot raise it from the floor. How can this be done by fraud with a table consisting of a top and four legs only? Again, a favourite test for visitors is to grasp the table while it is levitated eighteen inches up in the air and to try to prevent it reaching the floor again. This is impossible, as the table is pulled down so powerfully that a strong man cannot hold it back. *This experiment is impossible by fraud* under the conditions of the séance-room.

In Experiments 34, 35, 36, and 37 it is shown that I moved my arms, my hands, and rods freely below the levitated table and encountered no solid body whatever.

In Experiments 59 and 60 I moved apparatus freely in front of the medium between her and the table, and *I could plainly see the whole space and also the table.*

In general I have worked for the best part of a year below and round about the levitated table; I have explored the whole space surrounding it on many occasions; I have thoroughly observed by sight and by the use of instruments all that is to be noted; and I say now finally that every phenomenon occurring at the Goligher circle is absolutely genuine to the minutest detail. So conscientious are the medium and members of the circle that any accidental movement of the foot or body on the part of any is always immediately mentioned. It is, as I have said, a private family circle, and the greatest harmony exists amongst all the sitters. They have voluntarily allowed me to carry out the experiments without hope or thought of gain on their part, their idea being that since so many and such high-grade phenomena have been presented through them, they should do a little to help others not so fortunately placed;

and they consider they have done this by allowing me to experiment.

To Miss Kathleen Goligher, one of the greatest and best of physical mediums, I feel that it is necessary publicly to apologise for having, in her case, even to mention the fraud hypothesis. She knows, however, that I must do so. The truth, of course, is that nobody who has not visited the circle can have even the faintest idea of the magnitude of the forces involved, and the extraordinary variety and intensity of the phenomena produced. To all visitors the phenomena are so manifestly and palpably genuine that they are never troubled again with doubts as to whether there is such a thing as psychic force.

I will conclude my brief references to this matter by reproducing an article of mine from *Light*, written in reply to some of the usual sceptics who will believe nothing unless they themselves are witnesses:—

"Where was the Imposture, Conscious or Unconscious?

"I would like to say here that it is naturally repugnant both to myself and to Miss Goligher that any aspersions should be cast upon the genuineness of her mediumship. She is an upright and honourable young woman, has received no monetary recompense for what she has done, and has always been willing to give me her services freely in the cause of science. Her mediumship is absolutely beyond dispute, as many people, some of them well known, are able with certainty to say. However, she knows it is my duty to set at rest the minds of those who are afraid of unconscious mediumistic action and the like; of those who, not having been able to attend her séances and see for themselves what actually happens, wish to know what precautions have been taken, and what independent witnesses have to say.

"Fig. 1 represents in plan the following:—

"(a) The medium (M) and sitters (S . . . S) in position for the séance, the approximate diameter of the circle being 5 ft., the sitters seated on chairs; the medium seated on a chair placed on top of a drawing-board fastened to the platform of a weighing-machine. The square round the square for the medium represents the weighing-machine. X is my position with reference to the medium, close to her right side.

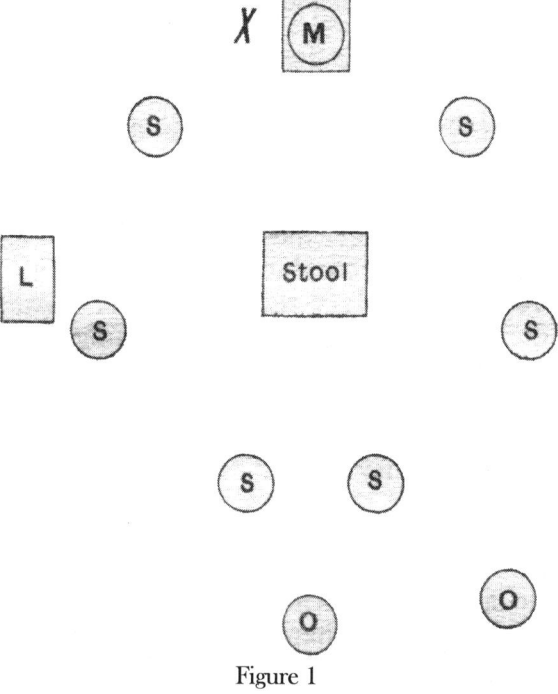

Figure 1

The weighing-machine was one of Avery's latest patterns, new, tested before being sent to me, tested by me before use, reading to 4 cwt., and sensitive to less than 2 oz.

"(b) The Light (L), an ordinary gas jet burning in a box behind red glass, the box being placed on a mantelpiece about 4 ft. high and in the approximate position shown.

The visibility was such that from my position I could clearly see each sitter.

"(c) In the centre of the circle the stool, with whose levitation we are concerned. It was a small wooden one weighing 2 lb. 12 oz.

"(d) Two observers marked O, O standing outside the circle, behind it, on the side opposite to me.

"*Time of Experiment:* About an hour from opening of séance, with psychic energy at a maximum.

"*Preliminary Arrangement:* Sitters unclasped hands and sat with hands on knees. Medium seated upright on chair on weighing-machine, with her feet close together on drawing-board (which was tied to platform of machine) and a hand, palm downwards, flat on each knee. Medium and machine completely isolated from other members of the circle. My instructions to her were to remain perfectly still. Having placed her in position, I carefully took the combined weight of medium, chair, and drawing-board. It was 9 st. 10 lb. 12 oz. The steelyard was just on the quiver. I placed the stool in the centre of the circle on the floor and came back and stood by the medium.

"*Instructions to operators:* To levitate the stool as high as possible and to keep it levitated until I desired it to be lowered.

"*The Phenomenon:* The stool immediately rose vertically into the air, until its height, at a conservative estimate, was 4 ft. above the floor. It obligingly rose just opposite the light, so that I could see plainly over it, beyond it on each side, and under it. I placed my head close to that of my medium, and saw that the legs of the stool were just about on a level with the top of her head.

"*Effect on the Weighing-Machine:* Immediately the stool levitated the lever of the weighing-machine rose with a click, plainly audible, against the top stop of the machine, indicating that the medium's weight had been increased. I adjusted the rider so that the lever again just balanced.

"*Control of Medium:* I placed my hand on the medium's right arm near the shoulder, passed it down her arm to her wrist, felt both wrists on her knees, and her knees and lower limbs perfectly still, as I had placed them. (The only difference was that her arms during the levitation were rigidly stiff—a characteristic of all levitations.) This I did two or three times. I could also, of course, see the medium, as, the stool being so small and so high in the air practically no shadows were cast. While I was doing this I kept looking at the stool, which remained nearly immovable about 4 ft. up in the air. While my hand was controlling her arm and knees, I carefully looked round every member of the circle and saw that all hands were accounted for, each on the owners knees. The nearest edge of the levitated stool was at least 3½ ft. from the medium's knees. It is to be remembered that the stool was floating on a level with the heads of the sitters.

"*Instructions to Operators:* When the stool had been thus up for about 1½ minutes, and everybody had examined it, I asked the operators to move it gently up and down in the air.

"*Effect on Weighing-Machine:* The lever went gently up and down against the stop in synchronism with the up-and-down movement of the stool. Everybody saw the up-and-down motion of the stool in the air quite plainly. Everybody could plainly see over, under, and all round the stool.

"The stool became steady in the air again. Finally, when I had examined it to my heart's content, and also the members of the circle and the medium, I asked the operators to lower the stool gently to the floor. This they immediately did, the stool slowly descending and softly touching the floor.

"*Effect on Weighing-Machine:* Lever immediately fell against bottom stop, indicating decreased weight of medium.

"Weighing-machine readings:—

Weight of Medium + chair + board
before levitation ....= 9 st. 10lb. 12 oz.
Weight of Medium + chair + board
during steady levitation ....= 9 st. 13 lb. 10 oz.
Increased weight of medium ....= 2 lb. 14 oz.
Weight of stool ....= 2 lb. 12 oz.

"*General:* The space between the medium and the levitated stool was not dark. I have been careful to understate rather than to overstate. I invite anyone to say where the fraud was in this particular case. If letters be kindly sent to me, care of Editor, I will go into any of the points raised. I would warn amateurs, however, that their explanations must cover at least 50 per cent of the facts, *including the results on the weighing-machine.*"

I wish to add finally that I fully satisfied myself, during each of the experiments described in this book, there was absolutely no fraud, and that the phenomena were due to the action of psychic force alone.

CHAPTER II

PHONOGRAPH RECORD OF THE NOISES

Experiment 1: Using a phonograph to verify the objective character of the noises.

A matter that required attention at the very beginning of the investigation was the question of the objective character of the phenomena. For one line of argument against the reality of psychic phenomena is to ascribe them to false sense-impressions received during a species of hypnotic trance induced by the peculiar conditions of the séance-room. Its advocates have it that the brain of man is so complex, so relatively unexplored, and so subject to deception, that it is incapable of dealing in simple fashion with psychic occurrences. In other words, the raps, knocks, levitations, and other manifestations are not objective but are hallucinatory effects produced in the subjective consciousness. This kind of argument, however, as the result of the great number of observations being continually made, and the commonsense of the people who make them, as well as by reason of our advance in the knowledge of the laws of hypnotism, is losing most of its grip. Almost everybody who studies psychic phenomena is convinced, by the evidence of his senses, of their objective reality. Various pieces of apparatus have been devised in the past to render this objectivity certain. Flashlight photographs have been taken of levitated tables. Movements due to psychic action have been recorded automatically. There is therefore little ground for any such hypothesis as that of collective hallucination. Nevertheless I thought it wise to perform one experiment to satisfy myself that the noises—raps, knocks, blows, shufflings, and so forth—were really objective sounds and not figments of the imagination. In order to accomplish this I made use of the phonograph.

I recognised that the taking of a satisfactory phonographic record would be a somewhat difficult matter, as the experimenter would have to submit to the hard-and-fast conditions of the séance-room, and would be unable, in any appreciable degree, to modify these conditions to his own advantage. I therefore called upon Mr. T. Edens Osborne, who deals in large quantities of phonographs, and who knows as much about such instruments as any man in Belfast, and together we made some experiments in a small uncarpeted room at the top of his premises. We found that with the phonograph on the floor (it was an Edison "Standard") rough imitations of raps made with the handle of a penknife came fairly clear, so long as the origin of the sounds was not more than a foot or so distant from the recording trumpet. We experimented for a considerable time, trying variations of height of the phonograph, and variations in character and position of the noises. Then I spoke a few words into the machine to the effect that I took the record (to follow) on 11th June 1915, and giving the name of the medium. This occupied only a short length of the cylinder, and the remainder was left blank.

The séance was held at eight o'clock on the evening of the date mentioned. The instrument was taken to the séance-room and placed on the floor in front of the séance-table, which was itself just in front of the medium (the table was afterwards removed). I placed some folded newspapers under it to deaden any vibration that might be caused by the more intense blows to be anticipated when the phenomena were in full operation. Then I inserted the cylinder above alluded to. The red gaslight was turned on and the séance commenced. In the usual way, slight raps were soon given in the vicinity of the medium, which quickly increased in intensity and volume. I may mention that the operators appeared to know all about this particular séance and its object, and had seemingly made preparations for it and were even keenly interested in it. At the suggestion of one of the circle, I explained to them the mechanism of the phonograph. This, however, did not appear to be altogether necessary. Then I asked for a rehearsal. This was immediately given—a little of everything in the way of knocks; and in addition, a small hand-bell was unexpectedly taken up and rung, which finally satisfied me that I had not much to tell the invisible entities as to what was required of them on this particular occasion. Then the question of time came in, and I found that the operators were not accurately able to gauge the minute and a half which was to be allowed them on each record. Accordingly, as a rough guide, a time duration of a minute and a half was measured to them by a watch. I then asked them to give a rap when they were ready for me to enter the circle (I recognised that I was ignorant of the psychic conditions obtaining within the circle, and I have made it an invariable rule always to let the operators arrange matters to suit themselves before carrying out an experiment, so long as the conditions I imposed were not broken). In five minutes or so, the summoning knock being heard, I moved into the circle, placed the recorder on the cylinder, and put my finger on the starting-lever. I then asked the operators if all was ready, and on their replying by three raps in the affirmative I called out, "Start." Immediately a thunderous blow resounded on the floor and I started the machine. Half a dozen sledge-hammer blows, varieties of double and treble knocks, and shufflings like sandpaper rubbing the floor were given in succession; the hand-bell was lifted and rung; the legs of the table were raised and knocked on the floor; the sound of wood being apparently sawn was heard, and so on. They kept up this terrific noise until I called out "Stop"; when, at the word, perfect silence reigned. We then tried the record, and found that most of the noises had been recorded; but the bell, owing to its being rung too far away, was almost inaudible. I therefore suggested to the operators that they should ring the bell right in the middle of the circle and as near the trumpet of the phonograph as possible, and I promised not to upset their conditions of equilibrium by attempting to touch it. Accordingly during the taking of the next record the bell was rung within an inch or two of my hand, and so close to the trumpet that it accidentally touched it and knocked it off the instrument. This partly spoiled the record.

In all, three good records and the partly spoiled one were taken, and these show beyond dispute, as was anticipated, that the sounds are ordinary objective sounds. Of course, the volume and intensity of the reproduced sounds are as nothing to the original ones, and the bell comes out only faintly; but they are all there, and on these four records we have, although in greatly diminished strength, nearly the whole gamut of phenomenal noises produced at the circle. The actual noises are said to have been the loudest ever given at the circle, and were heard quite easily two stories down, and even outside the house.

I append the following note by the Editor which appeared in *Light* of 7th Aug. 1915:—

"It will be remembered that in Light of June 26th last Dr. Crawford described an experiment in which he had taken phonograph records of the raps, bell-ringing, and other sounds produced at the séances for the physical phenomena which he is investigating. On Thursday 29th ult., Mr. Horace Leaf, who has recently visited Ireland, called upon us with one of the records kindly sent by Mr. Crawford, and this was tested on a phonograph—the various sounds (with the exception of the bell-ringing, which was very faint) being clearly audible.

"Dr. Crawford has thus proved to the satisfaction of himself and his fellow-investigators that the noises produced are objective sounds and not the result of collective hallucination—an important matter to the scientific investigator who desires to check his results at every step."

At lectures in Belfast and Dublin I have made use of the records for demonstration purposes. The sounds recorded are quite clearly audible in a hall holding up to five hundred people.

The matter is referred to in the following extract from the *Irish Times* of 18th March 1916:—

"A meeting of the Dublin Section of the Psychical Research Society was held on Saturday evening in the Mills Hall, Merion Row. The Rev. E. Savill Hicks presided. Dr. W. J. Crawford, of Belfast, gave a lecture on some experiments which have been conducted in Belfast during the past couple of years. He described how seven persons, all very religious people, sat from time to time in an attic, where there was no furniture but a plain wooden table and the chairs they sat on. The experiments had been conducted in good light and under the best conditions, and had been verified by instrumental means. A phonograph had been used to take a record of the raps that were heard on the table. (These raps were reproduced on an instrument here for the benefit of the audience.) The lecturer told how the table had been lifted and held suspended in the air for nearly five minutes, and how it defied the strength of a man to prevent the levitation. A stool had been lifted and a bell had been rung in the same mysterious way. Sometimes the 'raps' were as loud as the blows of a sledge-hammer, and could be heard outside the house. The object of the whole research, he said, was to find, if possible, the laws underlying the phenomena. Investigation had been going on for two years, and had not yet been concluded."

CHAPTER III

REACTION DURING LEVITATION OF THE TABLE

One of the first questions I asked myself when I decided to undertake a series of experiments was, naturally, the whereabouts of the seat of the reaction during levitation of the table. I had seen the table floating in the air, as it were, off and on for a period of over a year, and often I had wondered if the reaction was on the floor immediately below the table, or if it was on the medium herself, or if, indeed, it was located in neither of these positions. At that date I had not the slightest idea where I would find it, and any theorising I did usually ended in placing it in a different position on each occasion. Indeed, I did not desire to conceal the fact that even after eighteen months' observation I felt entirely ignorant of the mechanics of the whole phenomenon, the consequence being that I had at first to follow the "hit-or-miss" principle, trusting to luck that I might alight on something which would put me on the right track. I decided, therefore, that the best thing to do would be to seat the medium on the platform of a weighing-machine and see what would happen to her weight when the table was levitated. I did not know if the placing of the medium on the weighing-machine would inhibit the levitation, and I did not know at that period if the breaking of the chain formation of the circle, i.e. the unclasping of hands and placing them on the knees (for it is obvious that it would be useless to take readings of the medium's weight unless she was completely isolated from the sitters on each side of her), would likewise prevent the phenomenon. I had to trust to luck in these things.

Before describing as carefully as I can the experiments I made in an endeavour to ascertain the seat of the reaction, I will briefly state, even at the risk of recapitulation, the motions I have observed—and often observed—with regard to the levitated table. The table may be *steadily* stable, i.e. it may remain fixed practically immovable in the air without apparent support, for a minute or more. I do not think I have ever observed the table *absolutely* immovable over this period of time; there have always been minute movements and tremors in it; but for practical purposes it can be suspended, as it were, so as to be at rest. Then while levitated it can be moved up and down in a vertical line, and it can be moved to and fro practically horizontally (this latter motion is however, not exactly a true one in a horizontal plane, for the table seems to be moved more or less with its base as a pivot). Then the table may rock about in the air exactly like a boat pitching on a somewhat stormy sea, the analogy being so close that the observer can almost visualise the "waves" beneath it. There are also various other movements which I have often observed, such as a to-and-fro motion in the air with one end steadily tilted, and so on, but for the purposes of the experiments those mentioned above are the most important. And it is to be remembered that any of these various movements can be obtained at will, i.e. the experimenter has only to ask the operators for the particular motion he wishes, and it is given immediately.

The Apparatus: A platform weighing-machine; a drawing-board; some string; four tables.

The platform weighing-machine was kindly lent me by Messrs. W. & T. Avery, Ltd. It is known as the light, portable, platform type, and an illustration is given herewith (fig 2). It reads up to 4 cwt. and is sensitive to less than 2 oz., although the smallest movement of the rider is equivalent to exactly 2 oz. The machine was quite new, and was, of course, tested by the makers for accuracy before being sent to me. The dimensions of its platform were 22in. by 17in.

The drawing-board was an ordinary wooden one of half-imperial size, viz. 24in by 18in., about an inch thick. I placed this upon the platform of the weighing-machine, for I considered the dimensions of the platform were rather small for the work in hand.

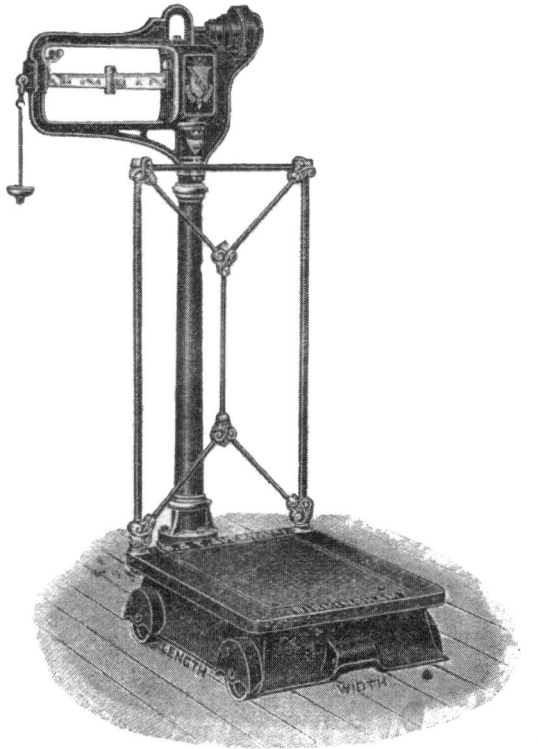

Figure 2

The string was used to fix loosely the drawing-board to the back-rail of the machine to prevent it falling if I required to move the machine about the room. The vertical distance from the floor to the top surface of the drawing-board was approximately 7 in.

The particulars of the tables used were as follows:—

Table 1: The ordinary rectangular deal séance-table; four straight legs; surface, 24in. × 17 in.; dimensions outside legs, 17½ in. × 15½ in.; height 2 ft. 5 in.; area of surface, 408 sq. in.; area of base, 271 sq. in.; weight, 10 lb. 6 oz. This was the table used for a variety of experiments besides the particular ones I am describing now, and when I henceforth refer to the séance-table I mean this one.

Table 2: Octagonal bamboo table; four legs; length of octagonal edge, 7½ in.; dimensions outside legs, 12 in. × 12 in.; height, 27½ in.; area of surface, 271 sq. in.; area of base, 144 sq. in.; weight, 6 lb.

Table 3: Bamboo table for holding ornaments. Besides the ordinary surface it had an underleaf for supporting a flower-pot; four legs; top surface, 17 in. × 17 in.; lower surface 9½ in. × 9½ in.; dimensions outside legs, 12 in. × 12 in.; height 2 ft. 5 in.; area of top surface, 289 sq. in.; area of lower surface, 90 sq. in.; area of base, 144 sq. in.; weight, 6 lb. 4 oz.

Table 4: More strictly, a rectangular wooden stool; four legs; surface, 12¾ in. × 13¾ in.; dimensions outside legs, 8 in. × 8 in.; height 11¼ in.; area of surface, 175 sq. in.; area of base, 64 sq. in.; weight, 2 lb. 12 oz.

The experiments on reaction were not completed at one séance, but were done in three stages at three different sittings; which method, it seems to me, is helpful in eliminating sources of error that might go undetected on any single occasion.

Method: I placed a table on the floor in the centre of the circle, and seated the medium on a chair placed on top of the drawing-board, which rested on the platform of the weighing-machine. Her feet were planted firmly on the surface of the board. The circle held each other's hands in chain order for half an hour or so with the object of allowing the séance to be well started and psychic energy to be fully developed. At the end of that time I asked the members of the circle to unclasp hands and to place them firmly on their knees. I personally placed the mediums hands squarely on her knees and saw that each sitter had his or hers similarly fixed. I told the medium to sit perfectly still during the experiment, and this she did, not perceptively moving throughout the tests. She was then physically isolated from all the members of the circle. During all the experiments I stood quite close to her at her right side.

I describe the tests from notes taken at the time. The reader must be prepared for a certain amount of recapitulation; but as experiments such as these on levitation under such ideal conditions can so rarely be carried out, and as therefore all details and data concerning them should in my opinion be carefully preserved, I do not think it is necessary to apologise. In other classes of scientific research I would not think of publishing details so much alike, but in psychic work we are far removed from all the ordinary scientific conventions.

Experiment 2: Reaction on the medium during levitation.

The table used was No. 1 (the ordinary séance-table). I accurately balanced the weight of medium, chair on which she was sitting, and drawing-board. The medium sitting perfectly still, I asked the operators to levitate the table and keep it as steadily levitated as they possibly could, i.e. without up-and-down or to-and-fro motion, while I was making my observations. Immediately on request the table rose about 8 in. into the air in an approximately horizontal plane (the levitations in general varied from about 8 in. to 12 in. in height, though in the case of the stool much higher results were obtained), and became to all appearance quite steady in the air. As soon as I was satisfied that all was right and that the medium was sitting perfectly still as I had placed her, I examined the weighing-machine. The steelyard, which before levitation was just on the balance, was now hard up against the top stop. I moved the rider along until it again just balanced. The following are the readings:—

Weight of medium + chair + drawing-board before levitation .... = 9 St. 4 lb. 14oz.

Weight of medium + chair + drawing-board during steady levitation ....= 10 St. 0 lb. 10 oz.
Increase in medium's weight due to levitation ....= 9 lb. 12 oz.
Weight of table ....= 10 lb. 6 oz.

Conclusion: The increase in weight of the medium due to levitation is 10 oz. Short of the weight of table.

Notes: The levitation was as nearly perfect as could be, and time was not a factor, as I had concluded my observations and there were no signs of the table descending. I had, in fact, to inform the operators that I had finished and to ask them to drop the table, which they did suddenly, so that it reached the floor with a crash.

Experiment 3: Reaction on medium during levitation.

The table used was No. 1 (the ordinary séance-table). The method was exactly the same as in Experiment 2, but the date was some weeks later. The following were the readings:—

Weight of medium + chair + drawing-board before levitation ....= 9 St. 4 lb. 0 oz.
Weight of medium + chair + drawing-board during steady levitation ....= 10 st. 0 lb. 8 oz.
Increase in mediums weight due to levitation ....= 10 lb. 8 oz.
Weight of table ....= 10 lb. 6 oz.
Weight of medium + chair + drawing-board at end of experiment ...= 9 st. 4 lb. 0 oz.

Conclusion: The increase in the mediums weight due to levitation is 2 oz. in excess of the weight of the table.

Notes: At the conclusion of the test it will be seen that I again took the dead weight of medium + chair + drawing-board, and that I found no alteration. There seems from this case to be no doubt that during levitation the medium increases in weight by an amount practically equal to the weight of the table. In Experiment 2 her increased weight was 10 oz. Short of the weight of the table. But during that experiment the full circle was present, and on this occasion Master Sam Goligher was absent on holiday; so that in the former case some or all of the 10 oz. may have been upon him, or the difference may have been due to experimental errors.

Experiment 4: Reaction on the medium during levitation.

The tables used were Nos. 1, 2, 3, and 4 in rotation, and the date was some weeks later than for Experiment 3. The method used was much the same, the only difference being that as soon as I had obtained the result for one table I removed it from the centre of the circle and placed the next in its place, and so on. The following were the readings:—

Weight of medium + chair + drawing-board before levitation .... =   9 st. 10 lb. 12 oz.

(It will be noticed that the medium was increasing in weight during the interval of about three months separating Experiments 2 and 4.)

Table	Description	Weight of medium + chair + board during levitation	Additional weight of medium due to levitation	Weight of table
1	Ordinary séance	10 st. 6 lb. 14 oz.	10 lb. 2 oz.	10 lb. 8 oz.
2	Octagonal Bamboo	10 st. 2 lb. 6 oz.	5 lb. 10 oz.	6 lb. 0 oz.
3	Ornamental	10 st. 2 lb. 10 oz.	5 lb. 14 oz.	6 lb. 4 oz.
4	Stool	9 st. 13 lb. 10 oz.	2 lb. 14 oz.	2 lb. 12 oz.

The dead weights given above for the tables were taken at the end of the séance, and tables 2, 3, and 4 agreed absolutely in weight with values obtained on previous occasions, while table 1 was on this occasion 2 oz. heavier.

Conclusion: The weight of each levitated table is practically added to the weight of the medium.

Notes: All the levitations were as nearly perfect as possible, and were maintained as long as I desired. I was not in the least hurried over my observations. The levitation of the stool was the most spectacular case of the phenomenon I have seen. So high was the stool in the air, it is no exaggeration to say that if I had bent my head I could have walked right under it from one side of the room to the other.

It is convenient to compare the results of Experiments 2, 3, and 4 by a percentage method.

Table	Weight of table	Additional weight of medium during Levitation	Percentage additional weight of medium to weight of table
1, Experiment 2	10 lb. 6 oz.	9 lb. 12 oz.	93.9%
1, " 3	10 lb. 6 oz.	10 lb. 8 oz.	101.2%
1, " 4	10 lb. 8 oz.	10 lb. 2 oz.	96.4%
2, " 4	6 lb. 0 oz.	5 lb. 10 oz.	93.7%
3, " 4	6 lb. 4 oz.	5 lb. 14 oz.	94%
4, " 4	2 lb. 12 oz.	2 lb. 14 oz.	104.5%

An average of the percentages in the last column of the tabulation gives for the six cases 97.3 per cent, as the percentage of additional weight of medium to weight of table.

The general conclusions from Experiments 2, 3, and 4 are as follows:—

A. When the table is steadily levitated, a weight is added to the medium very nearly equal to the weight of the table.
B. The seat of the reaction would therefore appear to be chiefly the medium herself.
C. Taking an average over the six cases, the increased weight on the medium seems to be about 3 per cent. less than the weight of the levitated table.

After having thus satisfied myself that the seat of the reaction was principally the medium, I wished to discover if the slight diminution of about 3 per cent in weight indicated in conclusion C was a real quantity or was simply due to experimental inaccuracies. First, let us take the sources of error likely to arise during the experiment.

(1) *Time:* There was no undue hurry in obtaining any result. The table was always levitated for a much longer time than I required to leisurely carry out the experiment. In fact, in all six cases I had to ask the operators to drop the table at the conclusion of the test. A levitation lasting from two to three minutes gives ample time to obtain a fairly accurate balance on a weighing-machine.

(2) *Errors due to Table moving about slightly in the air:* This is a positive source of error, and has to be guarded against very carefully. Every movement in the air of the levitated table causes an alteration in the weight of the medium. I will consider this point in more detail presently. Meanwhile it is sufficient to say that during the six levitations recorded above the table was as steadily levitated as could be. No doubt there were little jerks and tremors, for, according to my observation, it is impossible to have perfectly immobile suspension; but, if so, they were not apparent, and one could say that for all practical purposes the table was on each occasion perfectly at rest in the air.

(3) *Ordinary Experimental Errors:* These are fairly well guarded against by taking an average of several results. The question, then, as to whether the additional weight on the medium is a little less than the weight of the levitated table seems not so much a matter of experimental errors as of something due to some other cause. What this other cause is can be readily surmised. Do the other sitters in the circle, i.e. those exclusive of the medium, take any of the weight of the table? While most of the reaction undoubtedly finds its seat upon the medium, is there a small part located upon the other sitters? It is not an unreasonable supposition.

Accordingly I endeavoured to carry out an experiment to discover if there was any foundation for it.

Experiment 5: To ascertain if any of the weight of the steadily levitated table was added to one of the members of the circle other than the medium.

Method: I experimented with Mr. Morrison, whose place in the circle is on the immediate right of the medium. At nearly the conclusion of the séance I seated Mr. Morrison on the chair on the weighting-machine and the medium took her ordinary chair. All hands being on their owners' knees, he was thus isolated from the medium and from all the sitters. I carefully took his weight + weight of chair and drawing-board. Then, having carefully balanced the machine, I asked the operators to levitate the table steadily in the ordinary way. This they did. The following were the readings (the table was the ordinary séance one, weight 10 lb. 6 oz.):—

Weight of Mr. Morrison + chair + board before levitation ....= 10 st. 7 lb. 6 oz.
Weight of Mr. Morrison + chair + board during steady levitation...............= 10 st. 7 lb. 8 oz.
Difference ....= 2 oz.

The difference of 2 oz. here registered is too small for any conclusion to be drawn, but taken in conjunction with the following experiment would seem to place the result beyond dispute:—

Experiment 6: The result of experiment 5 being inconclusive, to see if a vertical motion of table in the air would have any effect on Mr. Morrison's weight while he was seated on the weighing-machine.

Method: With conditions as they were in Experiment 5, I asked the operators to jerk the levitated table up and down in the air, which they did. The steelyard of the weighing-machine previously balanced, went up and down lightly against the stops in synchronism with the movements of the table. I repeated the experiment several times until I was perfectly sure of the result.

Conclusion: A very small part of the reaction of the levitated table is located upon Mr. Morrison. By inference, therefore a small part of the reaction is located on all or on several of the sitters exclusive of the medium.

I therefore draw the complete conclusion from the results of Experiments 2 to 6, that when the table is steadily levitated, the reaction falls to the extent of at least 95 per cent upon the body of the medium, and that a very small proportion, not more than 5 per cent, is distributed over the bodies of the other sitters. As Admiral Moore suggests, when a table is steadily levitated the effect is precisely the same as it would be if the medium lifted it herself with her hands, aided by a very slight assistance from the members constituting the circle—say, the help that could be given by a force applied by one finger each. It is, however, to be remembered that Experiment 6 does not show absolutely that each member actually helps in the levitation. One or more of them may be neutrals. Experiments 2 to 5 have dealt with a system in equilibrium, i.e. with the table steadily levitated in the air and as nearly without motion as possible. It is evident, however, that the apparatus used in those experiments was quite suitable for obtaining results—not so accurate, perhaps, but nevertheless of much value—when the table was purposely given various motions while suspended in the air, or while it was moved in various directions along the floor. The following results, therefore, have to do with alteration in the medium's weight due to such motions. It is to be remembered that if the particular movement of the table desired by the experimenter was a possible one, it was almost always immediately given by the operators on request.

Experiment 7: The effect on the medium's weight of levitated table jerking vertically up and down in the air.

The table used was No. 1 (the ordinary séance table).

Method: The medium being seated quietly on the weighing-machine with hands on knees as in experiment 2, I asked for steady levitation of the table, which was immediately given. The weight of the medium + chair + drawing-board before levitation was 9 st. 4 lb. During the period of steady levitation the combined weight was 10 st. 0 lb. 8 oz. Having balanced the machine at this, I asked the operators to jerk the table (which up till then was steadily levitated) vertically upwards into the air. This they at once did, the table rising quickly from 6 in. to 8 in. into the air. I asked them to do it several times. The result was always the same. At each upward jerk of the table the steelyard of the weighing-machine rose and pressed against the top stop and then returned to its position of balance.

I also asked the operators to let the table slowly sag vertically in the air, and to arrest its motion suddenly before it reached the floor. This they did several times. I found that this motion also synchronised with instantaneous and temporary increase of the medium's weight due to steady levitation.

Conclusion: When the table is steadily levitated, the medium's weight is increased by an amount practically equal to the weight of the table. If the table is jerked up and down in the air, there is an additional instantaneous weight on the medium while the jerking is proceeding.

Experiment 8: The purpose was as in Experiment 7.

Method: As in Experiment 7.

The table used was the ordinary séance table.

The date of the Experiment was some months later than the date of Experiment 7.

While the table was being jerked up and down in the air, a temporarily increased weight (above that required for steady levitation) was on the medium.

Experiment 9: The purpose was as in Experiment 7.
Method: As in Experiment 7.
The table used was No. 4, the stool.

The stool being steadily levitated, I asked the operators to move it vertically up and down in the air, which they did. The lever of the weighing-machine, previously balanced for increased weight of medium due to steady levitation, went up against the top stop in synchronism, fell to bottom stop, rose to top stop again, and so on during the period of time in which the stool was in motion. The result was identical with the results of Experiments 7 and 8, although there was one point of variation in the method which was noticeable. It was this: The motion of the séance table (weight 10 lb. 6 oz.) caused vigorous temporary movements of the steelyard against the stops, while the motion of the stool (weight 2 lb. 12 oz.) caused movements which, although quite apparent, were feeble in comparison.

Besides the cases given in Experiments 7, 8, and 9, I have often at other times during my experimental work observed the effect on the medium's weight of tables 1, 2, 3, and 4 moving up and down vertically in the air. The result in all such cases was as stated above.

The following results arose out of the very complete Experiment 4. They were observed before and after the main results were obtained. Each was carefully verified at the time and on many subsequent occasions. I am designating each particular observation a separate experiment for the purpose of facilitating references.

Experiment 10: Movement of table along the floor.

At the commencement of the levitation experiments, the position of the table (No. 1) within the circle as I had placed it evidently did not suit the operators, for it was gently pulled along the floor until apparently the exact place desired was reached. The medium was at the time seated on the weighing-machine with hands on knees and body perfectly still, and the steelyard was balanced for her dead weight, weight of chair and drawing-board. While the gentle shifting of the table was in progress, the steelyard rose up against the top stop and remained there while the movement was going on, and fell as soon as it was over. This indicated, of course, that during the movement of the table along the floor the medium's weight underwent an increase. By my senses of touch on the end of the steelyard I judged that the increase of weight on the medium was from 3 to 4 lb., which would be about the magnitude of the force required to move the table along the floor against friction.

Experiment 11: Various movements of table.

The table used was the ordinary séance one (weight 10 lb. 6 oz.). I placed it on the floor within the circle. Having balanced the weighing-machine at the value due to the weight of medium + chair + drawing-board, I asked the operators to produce various movements of the table from slight shiftings and tiltings up to full levitation in order to enable me to note roughly the effects on the medium's weight. Results were as follows:—

(a) Table tilted steadily on two legs (two legs on the floor and two in the air): mediums weight increased.
(b) Table tilted higher than in (a): alteration in amount of increased weight.
(c) Table tilted with three legs in the air and one on the floor; further alteration in amount of increased weight.

For (a), (b), and (c) I did not read the values of the amount of additional weight on the medium, due to the tiltings, on the scale of the steelyard, but I balanced the steelyard on each occasion with the rider. None of these additional amounts of weights reached the magnitude of the weight of the table.

(d) The table was given translational movements along the floor; it was also moved rotationally 30 degrees or so over the floor; in all these cases the weight of the medium was increased during the time of the movement.

Conclusion: It is certain that each movement of the table produces increased weight on the medium, whether it be levitation, partial levitation, or movement along the floor; and with regard to movements which require a psychic opposition to the force of gravity, the increased weight may be anything up to the approximate weight of the table, according to the degree of levitation, whether it be partial or complete.

Experiment 12: Inference that levitation is in progress by observing the weighing-machine.

Having set the weighing-machine to balance at the dead weight of medium + chair + drawing-board, I several times purposely kept my eyes away from the table and fixed them on the steelyard of the machine. As soon as the steelyard rose against the top stop I would look around and either find the table levitated or partly levitated; i.e. by observing when increased weight was on the medium I was always certain by that fact alone to find a levitation in progress.

Experiment 13: Table tilted on two legs.

On one occasion at the end of a séance, the operators unexpectedly tilted the séance table on two legs and kept it in that position for a minute or so while the closing prayer was being pronounced. As the medium was at the time seated on the weighing-machine, I noticed that her weight, as evidenced by the steelyard pressing up tightly against top stop, was greatly increased, although I did not take the amount of the increase.

To find the effect on the mediums weight when the table was moved along the floor in given directions:—

Experiment 14: The table pulled along the floor towards medium.

Having balanced weight of medium, chair, and drawing-board as in previous experiments, I asked the operators to gently pull the table directly towards medium.

Result: While table was moving in towards medium from somewhere near the centre of the circle, the steelyard rose and kept pressed against the top stop, thus indicating that during that time her weight was increased.

Experiment 15: The table pushed along the floor directly away from medium.

Result: As in experiment 14, a continuous increase of weight of medium during the progress of the movement.

The general conclusion from Experiments 6 to 15 seems to be that all motions of the table whatever along the floor and all movements of the table in the air cause temporary increase of the medium's weight. In other words, forces which would be required to accomplish these movements are reflected somehow or other on the body of the medium.

The Distance of the Medium from the Table: I have already mentioned (Experiment 10) that the distance of the table from the medium seems to be an important factor during levitation. It is a mistake to assume that the closer the medium to the table the easier and quicker will the phenomenon occur. There seems to be a critical distance at which the best result takes place. For, under the mistaken notion that the closer the medium the better the result, I contracted the circle on several occasions when I required extra-powerful phenomena, i.e. I diminished the diameter of the circle by making the members sit closer together. But before any table phenomena occurred, the medium's chair (with the medium on it) was pulled or pushed back bodily along the floor for a distance of about a foot. This extraordinary phenomenon I have witnessed on many occasions. It tempts one to ask where the reaction can possibly be in such a case. I hope some time in the future to investigate it more fully.

On other occasions, with the normal diameter of circle, if the table happened to be too close to, or too far from, the medium, it would be pulled along the floor until the distance for levitation was apparently correct. I have witnessed this preliminary movement of the table along the floor dozens of times; in fact, it is not too much to say that it takes place just previously to every levitation, for the experimenter, when he places the table on the floor, hardly ever seems to strike the exact spot desired by the operators. As small a distance as an inch or two seems to make a difference.

I was rather amused on one occasion when I was engaged on some rather delicate levitation experiments. I was inside the circle as usual, and, thinking from long experience that the table was not just in the proper spot for the phenomenon, I moved it to the left for a distance of about six inches. No sooner had I done so than it was moved back by the operators to its original position. I thoughtlessly shifted it over again, and instantly it was again moved back. The fact was, of course, that the table happened in the first instance to be in the exact position desired by the operators, a thing which very seldom happened.

Conclusions: There is a critical distance in front of the medium, neither too close to her nor too far from her, at which levitation of the table occurs. If the distance is in the first instance incorrect, the table itself is moved by the operators if the disposition of the circle allows of it; and if the disposition of the sitters does not allow of it, the medium and her chair are moved back bodily.

The height of the levitation: The height to which a levitated table rises above the floor is important from several points of view. As in the case of the distance of the table from the medium, there appears also to be a critical height, which I should put, by rough estimation, at about 8 inches from the floor, whereat the expenditure of psychic energy is a minimum; for if levitation is asked for, I have noticed that the distance mentioned is the usual rise given, at any rate with tables weighing from 6 to 10 lb. But if a specially high levitation is demanded, or if the operators are giving an ordinary general demonstration, on which occasions they seem to desire to produce the most spectacular results possible, the height may be greatly increased, especially towards the end of the séance. On such occasions I have seen the surface of the table shoulder-high. However with high levitations there is not such a degree of steadiness as with low ones, the table generally twisting about with slow and sinuous motions this way and that. If we call the critical height about 8 in. for the ordinary séance table (as it appears to be), i.e. the height at which a steady levitation can occur with surface of table approximately level, then I have often noticed that if I ask, say for experimental purposes, a higher levitation than this, the operators seem to have to put forth a distinct effort. If success results, the table is jerked, not slowly raised, to the height demanded, and during the time it is at this extra height abnormal effort on the part of the operators seems to be necessary. The highest levitation I have ever seen was about 4 ft., which was the rise on one occasion in the case of table 4 (the stool, Experiment 4). It is certain that there is a maximum height beyond which levitation cannot occur; that maximum, so far as I have observed, being, as mentioned, about 4 ft., above the floor.

I have observed all sorts of freak levitations. For instance, on one occasion when the table had been levitated for about three minutes with the bottom of the legs about level with the knees of the sitters, the surface commenced gradually to incline about a horizontal axis, and continued to do so until it was nearly vertical; then the table moved over, in the air, to the chair where I was sitting, rested the lower edge of its surface on my knees, and then moved back and dropped to the floor.

Conclusion: There seems to be a critical height at which the operators can produce most easily levitation of the table—or at any rate a height at which they can obtain the steadiest and most prolonged form of the levitation. Anything above that height is a distinct effort.

CHAPTER IV

SOME MISCELLANEOUS EXPERIMENTS, OBSERVATIONS, AND CALCULATIONS

Experiment 16: Observation of levitation with calculation of upward pressure on under surface to account for it.

The table used was the ordinary séance one. Top surface 24 in. × 17 in.; height 2 ft. 5 in.; weight $10\frac{3}{8}$ lb.; material, deal (see Chapter III).

Time: Near opening of séance, with psychic energy not fully developed.

Commencement of Levitation: Table shook, rose on two legs, dropped and rose on the other two, dropped and rose on one, fell back on two, jerked rapidly about, and finally rose unevenly but completely into the air, the end which was lower being continually pushed upwards in order apparently, to get the surface level. After a little time the jerking ceased and table remained practically level and stationary in the air at a height of about 12 in. from the floor.

Duration of levitation: 4 minutes 30 seconds, during about 4 minutes of which time the table remained almost immovable in the air, a result evidently desired by the operators as indicative of their ability to maintain steady magnitude and direction of the psychic force. During the first minute of the time was taken by calling out the seconds, one, two, three, etc., by guesswork, and for the remaining $3\frac{1}{2}$ minutes or so by a watch; the error may amount to a few seconds.

The Psychic Pressure: The table during the greater portion of the levitation was practically stationary in the air, with its surface nearly level. If we assume that the levitation is effected by a uniform upward pressure on the under surface, we make the following calculations:—

SOME MISCELLANEOUS EXPERIMENTS

Weight of table .... = 10⅜ lb.
Area of under surface of table .... = 24 in. × 17 in.
.... = 408 sq. in.
Psychic pressure (approx) .... = 10⅜ ÷ 408
.... = 0.025 lbs. per sq. in.

This is of course a small pressure, and would be somewhat difficult to detect by mechanical means. For the sake of argument I am assuming that the pressure would be of the fluid type, though it is apparent that such a supposition is practically unthinkable. There is, moreover, good experimental reason to believe that the pressure, whatever its nature, is not applied to the table uniformly, but more or less over only a part of the under surface, evidenced, for instance, by the upward jerks given at any required corner during the commencement of levitation. Again the pressure may be applied at two or three places on the under surface, or the single area over which it is exerted may be capable of altering its location on the under surface in order to get the resultant under the centre of gravity. Or again, there may be no force on the under surface at all, and the table may in that case be supported by an upward force under each leg (although this hypothesis is rather extravagant), or it may be held in position in the air by rods projecting from the medium and gripping some part of the legs; or the levitation may even be brought about by an upward force from the top surface of the table. I mention all these suppositions so that the reader will understand I am not making assumptions light-heartedly. Each of them will be examined later on. Meanwhile the most reasonable hypothesis seems to be that there is some kind of an upward force below the surface of the table, and it is useful to make calculations accordingly.

Experiment 17: Observation of levitation with calculation of upward pressure on under surface to account for it.

The séance was held in my own house, in the drawing-room.

The table used was a square-topped one with four curved legs, with a lower surface near the bottom of the legs. During the evening it was levitated many times, the longest period being certainly well over a minute (although I did not time it).

Weight of table .... =   16 lb.
Dimensions of top surface .... =   20 in. × 20 in.
Height .... =   2 ft. 5 in.

The psychic upward pressure, assuming it to be uniform as in the previous case, would then be

$$16 \div (20 \times 20) = 16 \div 400$$
$$= 0.04 \text{ lb. per sq. in.}$$

It is therefore seen from the calculations that if we assume a uniform upward pressure on under surface of such tables as I have used in my experiments, the magnitude of that pressure is in all cases quite small, which fact I have found of some importance in working out the theory of levitation. The 16 lb. table of this test is the heaviest I have used during any of my experiments.

Experiment 18: Muscular force applied vertically downwards on top of levitated table.

During one of the levitations referred to in Experiment 17, near the conclusion of the sitting (with psychic energy therefore at a maximum), and with the surface of the table nearly shoulder-high in the air, I entered the circle and pressed down with my hands on the top of the table. Although I exerted all my strength, I could not depress the table to the floor. A friend who is over six feet in height then leaned over the circle and helped me to press downwards, when our combined efforts exerted to the limit just caused it to touch the floor. The kind of resistance encountered was an elastic one.

The table then stood up on two legs (with two legs in the air), and I used all my muscular force in an endeavour to depress the raised end, but I was quite unable to do so. It seemed as though a cushion of compressed air were below the raised portion.

It will be noticed that the levitation I have described in Experiment 16 occurred near the commencement of the séance, and that there was a considerable amount of preliminary jerking and jumping about of the table before true levitation of the table took place (i.e. the whole table at rest in the air, with no part of it in contact with the floor or with any solid object whatsoever).

According to my observations extending over two years, during which time I have seen hundreds of levitations under all conditions, levitations near the commencement of the sitting are nearly always of that type. It would seem that the psychic energy is not fully developed for half an hour or so after the opening, or at any rate that the operators cannot work so easily as they can at a later period of the sitting. About an hour from the commencement I have on many occasions had a series of ideal levitations, with no initial jerks or movements of any kind whatsoever. It would seem that in such cases the operators had their adjustments accurate and complete, and that they did not require any preliminary trials such as are common at the beginning of the séance.

The following is an exact account of ideal levitations I have on several occasions obtained near the conclusions of séances, with all conditions for the production of the phenomenon at their best, the mental harmony of the sitters perfect, their bodily health good, and all things seeming to flow with everybody and everything in the manner they sometimes do:—

(1) The table is stationary on the floor within the circle.
(2) I enter the circle and sit down beside the table.
(3) I utter the word "Rise" (or equivalent word or words).
(4) The table almost immediately rises three or four inches vertically into the air, without jerk or side movement or "fuss" of any kind, and remains fixed there without sensible motion (though doubtless there are a few unnoticed tremors)
(5) At the conclusion of the experiment, lasting perhaps half a minute, I utter the word "Fall" (or equivalent word or words).
(6) The table sinks gently to the floor.
(7) The processes (1) to (6) may be gone through half a dozen times in succession at intervals of a minute or two.

The reason for the instant response to the words "Rise" and "Fall" was because of previous arrangement with the operators, with the idea, on both sides, of economising words and explanations.

Experiment 19: The two kinds of resistance for a levitated table.

The table used was the one referred to in Experiment 17, and the séance took place in my own house. During one of the powerful levitations I entered the circle and stood over the table. Endeavouring to press it down vertically to the floor, I felt an elastic resistance, as already described. I then thought of pushing it inwards towards the medium. I was much surprised to find that the resistance to push in that direction was not an elastic one, but one of quite a different order. The resistance was a solid or rigid one, and, as a matter of fact, the table appeared to be "locked." As the results of this experiment are so important in the theory of levitation, it is necessary that the reader should be perfectly certain as to what I mean.

In figure 3, M is the medium, and T the levitated table. If the observer stands over the table and presses down in the direction A, he experiences a perfectly elastic resistance. If he presses in direction B, he experiences a solid and unyielding resistance. The actual direction of B I have not determined. It is not parallel to the surface of the table, but is downwards and inwards at some angle approximating to that shown. The direction probably varies somewhat with the height of the levitation. So solid and unyielding is the resistance in this direction that it gave me the impression that steel bars were connecting the table with the medium, and that I was pushing along the longitudinal axes of such bars.

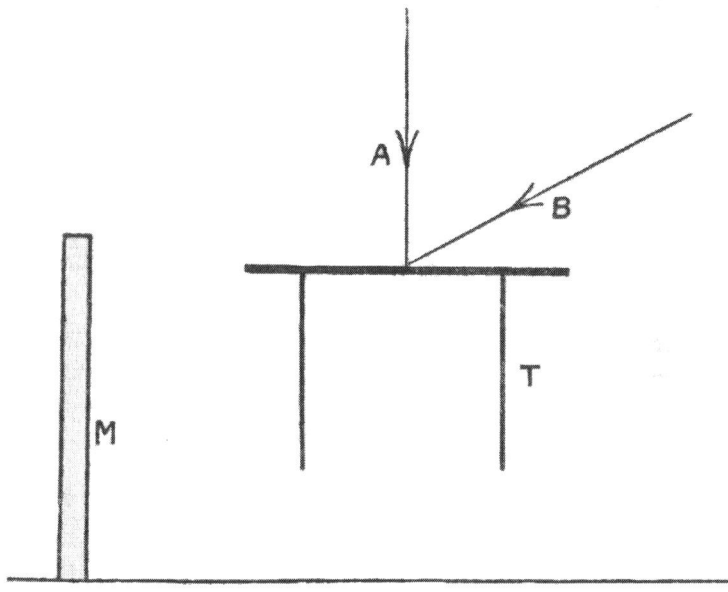

Figure 3

Experiment 20: Another test for the unyielding resistance of levitated table.

The table used was the ordinary séance one. I pressed inwards in a direction approximating to B (fig. 3), and again experienced the rigid type of resistance. It felt exactly as though I was pushing against a solid rod which had gripped the table from the body of the medium.

Experiment 21: Overturning the table to floor and raising it again.

The table used was the ordinary séance one. For ordinary experimental work it stands on the floor with its long edge parallel to the front of the body of the medium. The operators were asked to overturn it on to its side and to raise it into its normal position again. They first shifted the table round until its short edge was more or less parallel to the front of the body of the medium, and then they gently tipped it up on two legs and gradually turned it about these two legs until it lay on its side on the floor. The whole thing was done quietly and without fuss. Then the opposite process commenced. The operators endeavoured to raise the table into its normal position. But it was obvious this process was a difficult one, and there was nothing gentle about it, the table being given, apparently at the lower edge, what appeared to be sudden shoves and pushes, most of which were not successful (in the latter case the edge was only raised a little from the floor). Finally a shove more powerful than the others, or delivered at a better spot, accomplished what was required, and the table was again upright and standing on its four legs.

I have noticed that the table is, in this experiment, almost invariably turned over to the floor towards the left hand of the medium. I think there is a reason for choosing the left hand which I will refer to later on. I have observed the experiment at least a dozen times, and I saw it also on one occasion in my own house. We had formed an impromptu circle in a corner of the room. Only three members of the circle were present, including the medium. My wife, a young lady friend, and myself made up the circle, and a light bamboo table was placed in the centre. After a series of levitations, knocks, and so on, the table was turned over by the operators on its side, shifted about the floor until it was evidently just in the position required, then given one big heave which placed it upright on its feet. In this case there were no preliminary pushes or abortive shoves, for one movement accomplished the whole process.

Experiment 22: Increased and decreased weight of table standing on the floor.

While the table was standing on the floor, I asked the operators to increase its weight. This they immediately did, for on trying to lift it I found it impossible or nearly impossible to do so. The table seemed to be glued to the floor. Likewise, on asking the operators to reduce the table's weight I found I could lift it by a muscular effort of a few ounces. That is, the operators can apparently increase or decrease the weight of the table at will.

Experiment 23: Table levitated upside down.

This levitation was accomplished at the conclusion of a séance at which I was carrying out some experiments on phosphorescence, fluorescence, etc., for which purpose the room had been made perfectly dark. The levitation was therefore in complete darkness. So powerful was the levitating force that the table actually turned over and rose nearly a couple of feet into the air upside down, with the legs sticking upwards. I and three members of the circle each grasped a leg, and we tried to depress the table to the floor, but found it perfectly impossible. Furthermore, the table moved up and down and to and fro in the air with such powerful motions that we, who had hold of it, might as well have tried to stop the movements of a locomotive.

Experiment 24: Table on floor upside down. Visitor invited to raise it.

The ordinary séance-table, weight $10\frac{3}{8}$ lb., was used. It was placed upside down, and a muscular visitor to the circle was asked to catch hold of the legs and to raise it; he was unable to do so. I do not think I have seen anybody yet succeed in this attempt, and I have watched many try. The table seems to be glued to the floor, or to be held to the floor by some kind of suction between surface and floor, although this is not the correct explanation, as I shall attempt to show later on. This little test is really a most remarkable one, and most important and helpful in the forming of a satisfactory theory.

Experiment 25: Movements of table with experimenter sitting on it.

The table was standing on the floor. I sat upon it. The table was slid and jerked about the floor apparently with considerable ease, against obviously fairly large friction forces. I have seen many people other than myself sit upon the table and be thus moved about. A favourite experiment is to ask the visitor to sit steadily upon the table and to await calmly what shall happen. In a short time, usually inside a minute, the table gently rises upon two legs and slides him off to the floor.

Experiment 26: Position in which the operators like the table to be placed when they desire to exert the greatest psychic force possible on it.

I have watched the following process on many occasions. A visitor enters the circle and lays hold of the table, and is told by the sitters to do all he can to prevent it moving. If he is very muscular he may succeed for half a minute or so in preventing motion; but sooner or later, usually sooner, the table eludes him and gets into motion, jerking this way and that, levitating and dancing about in the air, and so on, and this in spite of the greatest restraining force he can exert.

Now, when such a visitor enters the circle, what usually happens is that the table, before he touches it, or by its first movement after he touches it, rises on the two legs remote from the medium and at an angle of about 40 degrees to the horizontal. It remains in this position for perhaps 10 seconds, and then immediately afterwards the tussle begins. This preliminary rising on two legs at the stated angle is no mere chance movement. It has a deep significance.

In fig. 4, M represents the medium and T the table tilted as explained. Does it not seem possible, nay, almost probable, that the reason for the initial tilt is to allow some projection from the medium to get the best grip possible on the under surface of the table, as indicated in the diagram? The object of the tilting would thus be to put the under surface of the table at the inclination most suitable for this projection to obtain the shortest and most powerful grip. The experimenter may stand anywhere round the table except directly before the medium, and not interfere to any extent with the intensity of the phenomena; but he may not stand *between* medium and table. I do not wish to say anything more definite than the above at this point, but I would, even at this stage, draw the reader's attention to the importance of the experiment.

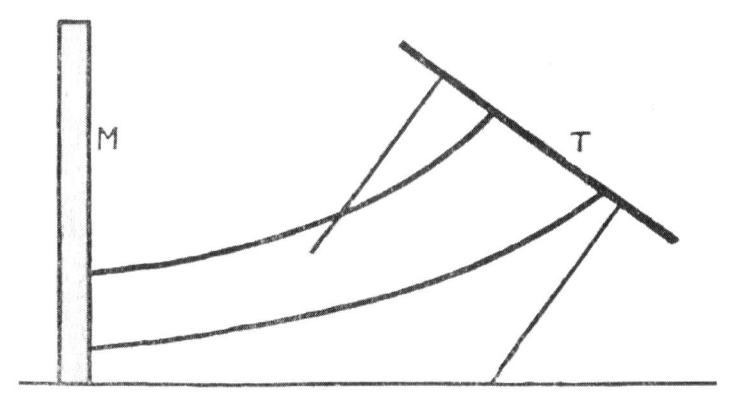

Figure 4

Experiment 27: Adjustment of levitating force to suit an unsymmetrical loading of table.

This experiment was not arranged by me, but was given spontaneously by the operators. I had brought a wooden box about 3 in. × 3 in. and 9 in. high, containing an electric bell and dry battery, which I intended to use for another experiment. The weight of the box, which I placed on the table near the edge, was 3.8 lb. suddenly levitation of the table unexpectedly began. Now, it was obvious that as the table weighed 10⅜ lb., and the box 3.8 lb., the centre of gravity of the two was some distance from the centre of the table. The operators, however, managed to keep the surface of the table nearly level, and they accomplished this by strong upward jerks if one of the edges sagged. They did not seem able to gauge the position of the combined centre of gravity with any accuracy, and so uncongenial did the uneven distribution of weight seem to be that they tried to jerk the electric-bell over to the centre of the table, but failed.

Experiment 28: To see if the operators could ring an electric bell.

An electric bell and dry cell were compactly fitted into a box (see Experiment 27), and the bell-push with contact button was fitted to the outside. The disposition of weight of the articles within the box, and the position of the push without, were so arranged that the bell could not be rung by human finger without knocking the box over; i.e. in order to ring the bell the box would have to be held. Furthermore the bell could only be rung by a force acting normally to button, for the wooden sleeve into which it fitted only allowed of in-and-out motion. Fig. 5 shows how the apparatus was arranged.

I placed the box on the floor near the medium, into what I conjectured was the strongest part of the psychic field. Then I asked the operators to ring the bell. After a little wait the box was shuffled here and there about the floor, then the bell was rung for an instant.

SOME MISCELLANEOUS EXPERIMENTS

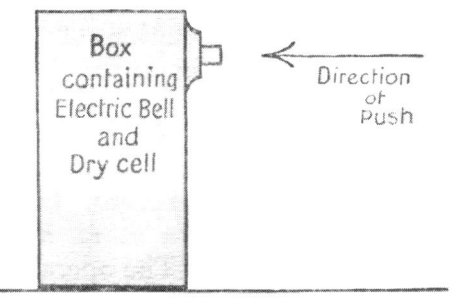

Figure 5

After a further wait it was rung again and for a slightly longer time. Afterwards it was more easily rung, and towards the end of the séance quite easily. The longest continuous ring was about 60 seconds. The box remained upright the whole time. I was rather surprised that the operators evidently found some little difficulty at first in ringing the bell, but the reason was at any rate partly apparent when I went into quantities. I found by experiment that the mechanical force required to cause electric contact was 0.8 lb. The area of the button was .246 sq. in., and (assuming uniform pressure) the psychic pressure was $0.8 \div .246 = 3.24$, say 3¼ lb. per sq. in., which was greatly in excess of the uniform pressure required to cause levitation of the table (the maximum value of the latter for my heaviest table was 0.04 lb. per sq. in.; see Experiment 17). A peculiar fact about this test was that while the bell was ringing, the push-button was not directly facing the medium, but was nearly opposite me, or perhaps at an angle of about 80° with the medium. The operators placed the box in this position themselves, so evidently it was in the most suitable place for the ringing of the bell. Perhaps the fact that, in order to prevent toppling over, the box had to be held from the back, had something to do with it.

Experiment 29: A small metal trumpet pulled when held in the hand.

The circle possessed for demonstration purposes, and for "direct" voice manifestations should such occur, a small conical metal trumpet about 18 in. long, open at both ends, about 2½ in. in diameter at the large end and ⅝ in. at the small end. (See Fig. 6.)

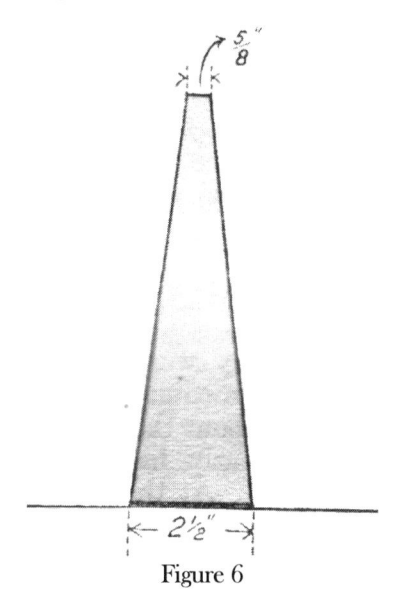

Figure 6

I held this small trumpet firmly by the hand at its small end, with the big end pointing into the air near the medium, at an angle of about 30° to the horizontal. I asked the operators to pull it. Nothing happened for some twenty seconds or so, and then suddenly it was given a strong forward jerk which almost snatched it from my grasp. Further trials gave similar results. The angular direction in which I held the trumpet seemed to make little difference.

Experiment 30: Attempt to prevent table returning to centre of circle from far end opposite the medium.

Sometimes the table would move of itself to the edge of the circle opposite the medium. I, sitting outside the ring of sitters, would then lay hold of it, and, exerting all my strength, would endeavour to prevent its return to the centre. I usually found this to be impossible. Some overwhelming force was evidently pulling in opposition—a force which appeared to be of the nature of a suction.

Experiment 31: A handkerchief placed on floor near medium.

I placed an ordinary white handkerchief on the floor near the medium, and asked the operators to move it about the room. Although I left it there for nearly half an hour it did not move perceptibly. At the time this seemed very strange, as one would naturally think that such a light article as a handkerchief could be easily moved about, when solid tables weighing over 10 lb. could be levitated and moved over the floor at a much greater distance from the medium. I think I now know the reason for this negative result, and I will refer to it later on.

CHAPTER V

CONDITIONS ABOVE, UNDER, AND ROUND THE LEVITATED TABLE

The experimenter, when he observes a table steadily at rest in the air, is confronted with a problem such as this: "How is the table supported?" There is obviously nothing material supporting it, for the space above it, underneath it, and all round, is empty of anything which in the ordinary course of events could keep it levitated. How then is the levitation accomplished? The obvious thing to do is to examine as carefully as possible the regions above, below, and all round the table in the hope that during the investigation some fact may be struck which may completely solve the matter by itself, or which in conjunction with other and allied facts will solve it. My method in this research was to get as many facts together as possible and to deduce the most likely solution from them.

The region above the Levitated Table: In my mind there is no doubt whatever that the region of space above the levitated table has nothing to do with the levitation; or if it has anything to do with it, it is only of very secondary importance. My reasons for this conclusion are as follows:—

(1) An experimenter may enter the circle, may grasp the table from the top, may sit upon it, and in fact may do practically anything he likes so long as he keeps his arms and body above the top surface.

(2) Fairly strong light may be flashed upon the top surface without affecting the levitation, while the same amount of light flashed beneath the table will immediately cause it to drop.

The operators have no objection whatever to the experimenter placing his hand anywhere he pleases on the top of the table, or he can place foreign bodies upon it, can rest a pocket lamp upon it, and so on.

The Region round the Levitated Table: There is only one place round the table which the observer may not cross, and that is the region between the medium and the levitated table. I myself many times while levitation has been in progress have moved inside the circle right round three sides of the table; and a visitor at an ordinary demonstration séance is allowed to walk inside the circle anywhere he pleases so long as he does not cross the line table to medium. In fact the instructions to the visitor are as follows: "Get inside the circle (two of the sitters raise their arms to allow him to slip under and in), grip the table from the top any way you please, and try to prevent it moving. You may move inside the circle anywhere you please so long as you don't get directly in front of the medium."

Therefore it is obvious that the only region of vital importance round the levitated table is that between table and medium. I will show later that the *whole* space between table and sitters has really some value—a very secondary one it is true, but nevertheless a real and substantial value,—and that, on occasions, some at least of this space, other than that in front of the medium, is made use of by the operators.

The Region below the Table: There is no doubt whatever that the space below the table is of prime importance to the levitation, and to movements of the table generally. I have many experiments to describe dealing with this region.

Conclusion: Thus, by a simple process of observation and deduction, it is easily seen that while a table is levitated the regions of space about it really vital to the phenomenon are the space between medium and table and the space beneath the table. All other regions are either of secondary importance or are of no importance at all.

Experiment 32: A fairly strong light placed on top of the levitated table and on leaf under top surface.

I took a pocket electric flashlight, covered the lens with a few thicknesses of thin red tissue paper, and placed the lamp upright on the levitated table. There it remained while the table moved gently up and down in the air, for quite a minute. On another occasion, when the battery was quite new, and the lens was covered only with two thicknesses of the thin red paper, I placed the lamp on the table before levitation, and then asked that levitation should be given. This, however, proved to be impossible. The light was too strong, and was shining too directly upon the medium. Generally speaking, it may be said that small concentrated sources of light close to the medium are bad for phenomena, but that a diffused light from some distance away, whose source is not concentrated but spread over a large area, such as a flame surface, is least inhibitive. When the table failed to levitate with the electric lamp standing vertically, I placed the lamp flatwise on its side on the table, with the lens end pointing away from the medium, when levitation immediately occurred and was kept up for a long time. The table had a lower leaf (the séance was held in my own drawing-room) about 9 in. from the floor, and the lamp was then placed on this flatwise, with illuminated end pointing away from the medium. After a little while the table was again levitated, and remained so for a fairly long time, although there seemed more difficulty in starting levitation with the light placed thus than when it was on the top surface. This would indicate that it is the lower portion of the body of the medium which is most concerned in the phenomenon. These experiments also show that it is the end of the table nearest the medium and the region under the table near her that are affected during levitation.

Experiment 33: The table being steadily levitated, to discover what effect is produced on the levitation by sliding a body of considerable volume under the table.

The table used was the ordinary séance one. When it was steadily levitated, I gently moved a spring balance of the compression type 8½ in. high, and with a rectangular top surface 8 in. × 6 in. along the floor until it was underneath the table. No part of the balance was in contact with the legs or with the under surface of the table or any part of it at all. There was a clear space of at least 18 in. between the pan of balance and under surface of the table (the reason I used a balance rather than a small wooden box or anything else, was because the balance was handy, as I was that evening doing other experiments with it). There was a positive result. The table, which before the experiment, was tranquil a few inches up in the air, fluttered (that is the only word which describes its motion) like a wounded bird and dropped gently to the floor.

Conclusion: The space displaced by the balance is a factor in the levitation, and the levitation is in effect produced by some kind of an upward force upon the under surface of the table; also, the region somewhat near the floor beneath the table is of importance in the production of the phenomenon.

Generally speaking, for the production of good phenomena the space underneath the table must be kept relatively darker than the rest of the room. This, in the case of the larger tables, is accomplished automatically, for the comparatively large area of surface places the under region in shadow. Therefore this region is the most troublesome to deal with throughout the whole room. Nevertheless the light is strong enough for most purposes; and although scale readings cannot be obtained by sight, the sense of touch can be called in, as will be explained hereafter.

In order to discover, if possible, the kind and position of application of the supposed upward force applied to the table to levitate it, I performed a number of experiments which I shall now describe.

Experiment 34: Exploring the region under the legs of the levitated table by the hand.

The table used was the ordinary séance one, which weighs about 10½ lb. If the upward psychic force was exerted upon the bottom of the legs only, and not upon the under surface, there would be an upward force upon each leg of (10½ ÷ 4) lb., say about 2½ lb. If a hand be placed under a leg with, say, palm upwards, it is reasonable to suppose that the reaction of 2½ lb. immediately under the leg and exerted upon the palm of the hand would be perfectly apparent. To test this, then when the table was steadily levitated I placed my right hand upon the floor, palm uppermost, immediately under each leg in succession keeping the hand in each position for five or six seconds. (While carrying out these experiments I may mention that I was sitting inside the circle beside the table on the side remote from the medium; my reason for this particular position being that I might not disturb the field between medium and table.) The result of this experiment was entirely negative. I felt not the least sign of pressure upon my hand when it was under any of the legs, or when I gradually raised it from the floor till it touched the bottom of the legs, which would indicate that the phenomenon of levitation is not produced by an upward force on each leg, or, if there is such an upward force, it is a small one and only subsidiary to the main levitating force.

Experiment 35: Exploring the region under levitated table by the hand and arm.

If we suppose that the levitation is produced by a uniform upward pressure upon the under surface of the table, we find, from dividing the weight of the table by the area of its surface, that this upward pressure, in the case of the séance-table, would amount to 0.025 lb. per sq. in. (see Experiment 16). During steady levitation, I placed the back of my open hand with palm presented to the field (a) upon the floor in various places under the table, and (b) upon the under surface of the table, but I experienced no sense of pressure anywhere. As, however, a pressure of 0.025 lb. per sq. in. over the few square inches of the palm would amount to very little, this result is not to be wondered at.

I put my arm right underneath the table from end to end near the floor, moving it gently to and fro, but I experienced, as before, no sense of pressure anywhere.

The general conclusion from Experiments 34 and 35 seems to be that the table is not levitated by means of forces applied under the legs only, for the forces would be comparatively large in that case, and the mere fact of the hand moving up from floor to bottom of the leg would certainly interfere with the levitation (see Experiment 33). This would still be the case if we are to suppose that psychic force cannot act on the bare human hand, owing, let us say, to some kind of an aura surrounding it which neutralises its effects. So it is pretty evident that any theory which bases levitation upon vertical upward psychic force upon the bottom of the legs is untenable. There is a special reason why no force should be felt on the hand when the latter is on the floor under the levitated table, which I shall deal with later on. Why there should be no sense of pressure experienced when my hand was touching various places on the under surface of table may be due to the following reasons:—

(1) The upward force was too small in magnitude.

(2) The upward force was actually present, but owing to an aura from the hand (or hand and arm) the psychic force was neutralised over the hand, and was slightly increased in magnitude over the rest of the under surface in compensation, with the consequence that the table remained levitated. The volume of the hand and part of the arm beneath the table was probably too small to seriously interfere with the levitation (see Experiment 33).

Experiment 36: The effect of crossing the space beneath levitated table with a thin glass tube.

The table used was the ordinary séance one. When it was steadily levitated I took a thin glass tube, about ⅜ in. outside diameter and about 14 in. long, and, grasping the end of it in my hand, I moved it about below the table at various heights. Then I made a wide sweeping movement with it immediately under the legs, and beyond the base of the table on all sides, stretching my arm until the end of the rod came into contact one by one with the feet of the sitters.

During this process the levitation was unaffected.

Conclusion: A body of small area and bulk may be inserted below the table while it is levitated without affecting the phenomenon. I have, however, reason to believe that this is not generally true, but only true when the levitation is a powerful one. To an uninstructed observer it might appear that there cannot be such a thing as reserve of force with regard to a levitated table, i.e. that a force of exact magnitude is required for the phenomenon, neither more nor less. But such a view does not go far enough. Sometimes there seems to be just sufficient force exerted to keep the table levitated and no more, in which case any disturbance, such as a hand being placed beneath it, causes it to drop; at other times, and most often, there seems to be a reserve of force to draw upon, so that there is immediate compensation for any small disturbance, and the table remains in the air.

Experiment 37: Exploring the region of space beneath the levitated table with a manometer.

Fig. 7 shows diagrammatically the main portions of the instrument.

A is a U-tube of glass, connected to a straight tube of glass by a small piece of thick rubber tube at B. The free end of C is turned up at right angles. Both ends of the apparatus X and Y are open to the atmosphere. A is half filled with water, and when there is equal gaseous pressure at X and Y the water remains at the same level in both limbs of the U-tube. If, however there is greater gaseous pressure upon Y than X, the water rises in the left-hand limb of the U-tube and falls in the right-hand one, and the difference of heights is a measure of the difference of pressure. The length of the tube C was 14½ in. Fig. 7 shows the elements of the apparatus only. As a matter of fact, the manometer used was a fine instrument required for measuring the pressure of the gases in steam boiler flues. It has a cock which can be rotated by finger and thumb, so that the gaseous pressure can be held at any instant, and thus the difference in heights of the columns of water examined at leisure.

If we suppose that there is an uniform upward pressure of 0.025 lb. per sq. in. under the table, and if we further suppose that this pressure is exerted by something of the nature of a gas, and that this gas is contained within limits beneath the table (although such suppositions appear unthinkable), then we might expect to see a difference of pressure indicated on the manometer of about 0.7 in.

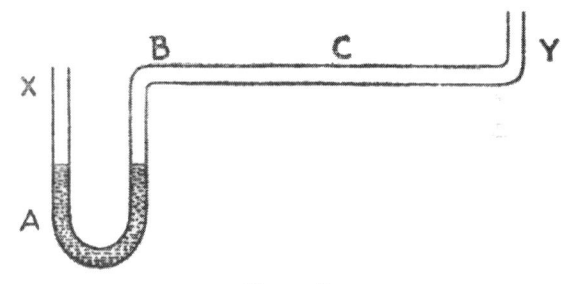

Figure 7

During periods when the table was steadily levitated, I inserted the end Y of the manometer, with this end always pointing vertically upright, (a) immediately under a leg of the table, (b) at various places near the under surface of the table, (c) at several points in space between the floor and the surface of the table. The placing the tube in these positions in no wise affected the levitations. When I had held the tube in any one of the above-mentioned positions for a few seconds, I turned the tap (which would hold the gaseous pressure if such was there, and thus keep the difference in columnar heights of the water fixed), removed the instrument from below the table, and examined it in strong light. The results were entirely negative. There were no indications of difference of gaseous pressure anywhere.

Conclusion: It would appear from this experiment that the levitation is not due to the static pressure of a fluid.

The results of several of the previous experiments gave me some reason to think that on the floor or close to the floor beneath the levitated table there might be a reason where there was no psychic force acting, or that the levitating force was confined, as regards space, to a location just under the surface of the table. The question uppermost in my mind was: "Is there a direct reaction upon the floor, or does the region of psychic force end above the floor?" It is very natural so suppose, of course, that there is some kind of a field extending between the under surface of the table and the floor immediately beneath, and that there is a direct stress across this medium. The hand might not be a sufficiently delicate instrument for cognising such a reaction supposing it to be in reality present, or there might be something about the human hand, such as an aura or an emanation, that would neutralise or nullify the action of psychic force in its vicinity. For a long time, so ignorant was I of the mechanics of the whole phenomenon, I was fully under the impression—or delusion, as I now know it to have been—that there was direct reaction on the floor under the levitated table.

Experiment 38: To discover if there is a reaction upon the floor or in the immediate neighbourhood of the floor under a levitated table.

The apparatus consists of (1) an electric bell and wires; (2) a dry battery; (3) the bell push with button removed; (4) a piece of thin wood 5 in. square, with a small circular piece let into it at the centre which took the place of the button of the push.

In Fig. 8, A is the elevation of the thin piece of square wood, B is the circular piece fixed to it, C is the bell-push, W the wires running to the bell and battery. A piece of rough red cloth was tacked to the top of A, for I had found from experience that a piece of course coloured or dark cloth fixed to anybody which is to be acted on by psychic force facilitates the application of the force. The piece B rested on the top contact of the bell-push, and the consequence was that, when a slight downward force was applied to any part of A, electric contact was made and the bell rang. I so arranged matters that the weight of even the little finger resting on any part of the surface of A caused the bell to ring. The total height of the apparatus when it rested on the floor was not more than 2 in.

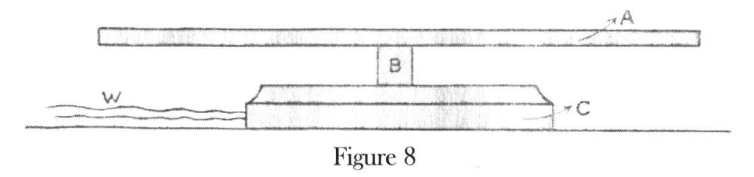

Figure 8

Method: The table used was the one in my drawing-room, weight 16 lb., and the séance was held in my house.

Fig. 9 shows a rough sketch of it, levitated about a foot above the floor. It is to be noted that this table has a lower leaf as shown. When the table was levitated I slid the pressure apparatus along the floor, to and fro, here, there, and everywhere beneath the table. (The bell and battery were outside the circle.) The result was that while the mechanism was beneath the table the bell did *not* ring.

Conclusion: There is no reaction on the floor beneath the levitated table. This is a most important result—so important, indeed, that I have verified it completely by three other experiments (Experiments 51, 52, 61), which I do not describe here as they fit in better in connection with other and somewhat different tests. It will be seen that the question of a human hand with its possible aura does not come in here; the reaction, had it been present, would have been exerted on a wooden surface covered with a rough cloth—the best kind of surface, as experience shows, for the application of psychic force.

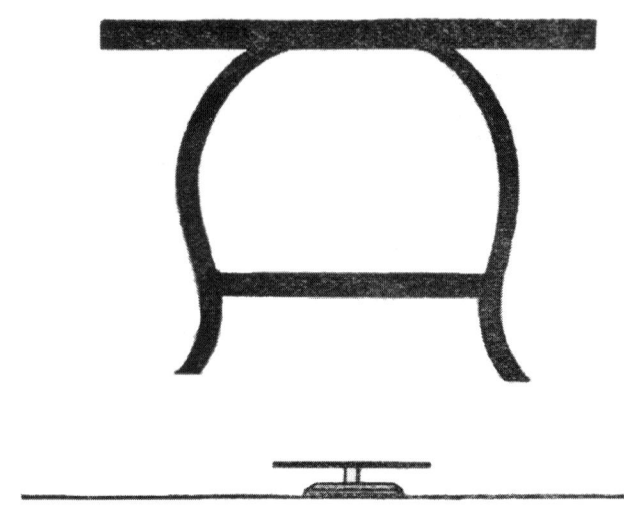

Figure 9

That the operators could make use of the pressure apparatus, and that the bell would have rung vigorously had there been the smallest psychic reaction upon it, is seen from the following experiment.

Experiment 39: To see if the operators could use the apparatus of Experiment 38 to ring the bell by the direct action of psychic force upon it.

I placed the apparatus on the floor away from the table, and asked the operators to reply to questions by ringing the bell instead of by their customary manner of raps on the floor. Immediately on request the bell was rung, and from then to the conclusion of the séance the operators communicated in that manner (and seemed, indeed, rather to enjoy the change). Likewise they wished us good-night by long rings on the bell instead of by their usual method of raps.

CHAPTER VI

LEVITATION DIRECTLY ABOVE THE
PLATFORM OF A WEIGHING MACHINE

Before I came to the conclusion that during a normal levitation above the floor there was no reaction or pressure upon the floor under the table, I was of the opinion, as I have already mentioned, that some kind of equilibrium was established between the medium and the table involving a reaction upon the floor. This view, which I now know to have been erroneous, was nevertheless a fortunate one for me to adopt as it turned out, because I thereby learned, by experimental work, much more about the mechanism of levitation than I otherwise would. My purpose in this chapter is to describe and discuss experiments I carried out in which I obtained levitation immediately over the platform of the Avery weighing-machine (the machine already described in Chapter III).

It will be remembered that the dimensions of the platform of this machine were 22 in. × 17 in. The ordinary séance-table measured 24 in. × 17 in., and round the legs 17½ in. × 15½ in. In order, therefore, to increase the effective area of the platform the drawing-board already mentioned (see Chapter III), 24 in. × 18 in., was tied to it.

Experiment 40: Preliminary trial of apparatus to see if the operators were likely to be able to carry out the required levitations.

This test was carried out with only four of the members of the circle present, the medium being included.

Fig. 10 shows the essential arrangements. A is the platform of the machine, B is the drawing-board fixed to platform, C the back rail of machine, and D the table standing on drawing-board. The position of the medium throughout these tests is indicated by the letter M, the front of her body being parallel to the long edge of the table, and

LEVITATION OVER PLATFORM

she sitting on her chair looking *across* the platform and not at the back rail.

The weight of the drawing-board................... = 5 lb.
The weight of the table .... = 10 lb. 6 oz.

The table having been placed neatly on the board, the séance opened.

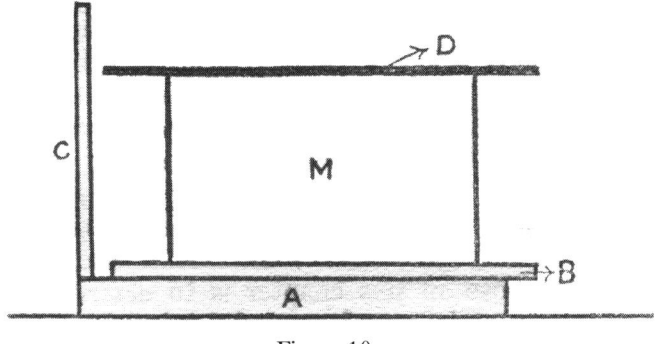

Figure 10

The machine was balanced for the total weight of table + drawing-board, viz. 15 lb. 6 oz. After some time two legs of the table were lifted up into the air, the other two remaining on the platform. The steelyard immediately went hard up against the top stop, indicating a greatly increased weight upon the machine.

(a) During one particular tilting (there were several of them) I balanced the steelyard at about 26 lb. Now the dead weight being 15 lb. 6 oz. and the table still resting on two legs on the platform, it was obvious that some kind of a force much in excess of that due to direct reaction was in operation.

(b) In another case of tilting, the weight registered on the machine was greater than 26 lb., though I did not actually measure it.

I got the impression, from observing pretty carefully some half a dozen cases of tilting at various angles, that with increasing height of raised end an increasing weight was put on the machine. Complete levitation did not occur. It seemed to me that the mere fact of partial levitation caused an extra back pressure, as it were, on the platform, a pressure that was always greater than the static load of 15 lb. 6 oz.

From the result of this experiment it seemed to me likely that with the full circle present complete levitation would be obtained. Accordingly the next test was carried out with the full circle present.

Experiment 41: The séance-table being levitated directly over the platform of the weighing-machine, to measure the reaction on the platform.
Weight of table ....= 10 lb. 6 oz.
Weight of drawing-board............................= 5 lb. 0 oz.
Total dead weight ....= 15 lb. 6 oz.

The table was placed symmetrically on the drawing-board and the séance commenced. With the table in position there was only an inch or two of space outside the legs, and thus very little room for side play or for manipulation. The steelyard was balanced for the dead weight of 15 lb. 6 oz.

(A) Within a few minutes psychic force was being somewhere applied to the platform, for the steelyard was oscillated to and fro against the top stop. The table also jerked about on the narrow platform, and now and then an end was slightly raised but quickly lowered. This sort of thing continued off and on for a quarter of an hour or so, and I was beginning to think the operators would be unable to effect the required levitation. Then I heard seven or eight raps on the floor in succession, the prearranged signal that they wished to give a message. By means of raps the following was spelt out; "Cover the drawing-board with a dark cloth." Now the drawing-board was white in colour, the original wood not having been varnished or touched in any way, and the trouble was apparently due to some kind of reflected white rays coming from its surface (see Experiment 31). The circle was accordingly broken for a few minutes while one of the members went downstairs for a thin piece of dark cloth, which was placed over the drawing-board. Its weight being only an ounce or two, did not materially affect the dead load. The experiment now proceeded much more successfully. The table was again oscillated on the platform, and was then lifted on two legs (two legs thus remaining on the machine and two in the air above it).

(B) This lifting coincided with a large apparent increase of weight, as much as 14 lb. Additional to the value of the dead load being registered (compare Experiment 40). Several times was an end of the table thus raised, and on each occasion the sudden corresponding increase of weight, varying from a few pounds up to a maximum of about 14 lb. was noted. Complete levitation did not occur until about forty minutes after the opening of the séance, and then it only lasted for four or five seconds and was of a rather jerky type. (It was very evident that the phenomenon could only be produced with difficulty, owing chiefly, I believe, to the close approximation of areas of base of table and of the platform, which allowed of very little manipulation.)

(C) But immediately it occurred, the registered weight, which was the previous instant several pounds above the dead-load value of 15 lb. 6 oz. (due no doubt to the preliminary tilting just before levitation, see Experiment 40 and (A) and (B) above), came back, and the steelyard balanced at something like the original load. During the next few minutes levitation took place several times, on each occasion increasing in duration and steadiness. At length almost perfect levitation, about 6 in. in height, was obtained, lasting for fully half a minute, with the surface of table almost level, and the table nearly steady and just covering the platform. With the exception of one case to be described later, it was the most wonderful levitation I have witnessed in the course of my investigation.

(D) Immediately it occurred the steelyard balanced at about 15 lb., oscillating a pound or so on either side of this, in correspondence, apparently, with the slight up-and-down tremors of the table in the air.

Conclusions: (1) With table tilted—only half levitated ((A) and (B) above)—there is on each occasion a reaction on the machine many pounds greater than the static load, and the magnitude of this reaction varies in some manner with the height of the tilting. This agrees absolutely with the result of Experiment 40.

(2) During fairly steady levitation the reaction of the levitated table on platform is apparently nearly equal to the weight of the table (see (C) and (D) above).

(3) The movement of the table up and down in the air above the platform causes variations of a few pounds in the reaction as measured on the weighing-machine.

Experiment 42: Levitation of table No. 2 over platform of weighing-machine.

At the conclusion of Experiment 41, I removed the ordinary séance-table—which, on account of its nearness in size to the platform, required most careful manipulation and was on that account difficult to levitate—and placed a smaller bamboo table (table 2) on the platform of the machine. The base area of this was much less than the other table, and there was consequently more room round it on the platform. I then balanced the steelyard for dead weight of table and drawing-board.

Weight of table .... =	6 lb.
Weight of drawing-board .... =	5 lb.
Total dead weight .... =	10 lb.

The séance was now near its conclusion and the psychic energy available was evidently at a maximum, for no sooner had I placed the table on the platform when it immediately rose into the air, and the levitation could apparently have been kept up for several minutes if I had desired it.

(A) With the exception of variations of a pound or so, which seemed to correspond with small up-and-down jerks of the table in the air, the steelyard remained balanced as for the initial dead load of 11 lb. I watched with interest the small variations in registered weight, balanced by moving the rider a trifle this way and that, as the table sagged a little or was raised a little in the air.

Conclusion: As in Experiment 41, the reaction on the platform of the weighing-machine appears to be about equal to the weight of the levitated table.

Experiment 43: About a month after the date of Experiments 41 and 42, I carried out further similar tests on two more tables: (a) the ornamental bamboo table and (b) the stool (tables Nos. 3 and 4).

Weights:—   Table 3 = 6 lb. 4 oz.
                  Table 4 = 2 lb. 12 oz.

With table 3 the levitation was prolonged, quite steady, and of average height of about 7 in. The surface was not level but was inclined at an angle of about 30° to the horizontal, the lower edge being towards the side of the platform farthest from the medium. When equilibrium was established, with the table steady in the air, the weighing-machine registered (subtracting the dead load of drawing-board) a reaction of about 13 lb. 6 oz., or more than double the weight of the table. But it was noticeable that the steelyard was just a little stiff, as though there was a side thrust somewhere on the mechanism supporting the platform.

With table 4 (the stool) the levitation was also very good and prolonged, and of an average height of 9 to 10 in. The surface was also in this case inclined at an angle of about

30° to the horizontal, the sagging edge as before being farthest from the medium. A very heavy reaction was registered on the weighing-machine, and the steelyard was quite stiff. The average reaction (between weight needed to allow steelyard to rise and that necessary to cause it to fall) was no less than about 31 lb. 10 oz. (excluding weight of drawing-board). As soon as levitation was over, the machine instantly regained its usual sensitiveness. The following tabulation will enable results to be compared:—

Experiment No.	Table No.	Character of levitation	Weight of Table	Reaction due to levitated table (about)
41	1	Level	10 lb. 6 oz.	10 lb 8 oz.
42	2	Level	6 lb.	6 lb.
43	3	Inclined at about 30° to horizontal	6 lb. 4 oz.	13 lb. 6 oz.
43	4	Inclined at about 30° to horizontal	2 lb. 12 oz.	31 lb. 10 oz.

In all cases I had plenty of time to make my observations, and I believe the results are accurate. With tables 1 and 2 I did not notice any loss of sensitiveness of steelyard while measuring the reaction, but with table 3 there may have been a slight loss, and with table 4 there was certainly a great loss.

General Conclusions from the Four Levitations: The results given above in the tabulation are, or were at the time I obtained them, extremely puzzling. The following are some observations I made at the time:—

It would seem that when the table is comparatively large—i.e. when its surface and base area bear some resemblance to the area of the platform—the reaction is practically equal to the weight of the table. (In the light of later and different experiments I do not now think this statement is altogether accurate. I now know that the height of the platform above the floor is the all-determining factor.) A rough comparison may be helpful. The area of the platform is 432 sq. in. The area of the surfaces of tables 1 and 2 are 408 sq. in. and 271 sq. in. respectively and their heights 29 in. and 27½ sq. in., and in each of these cases the reaction is about equal to the weight of the table. In table 3 the area of the lower surface (there are two surfaces in this case, and it is reasonable to suppose that it is the lower one upon which the psychic pressure is exerted) is 90 sq. in., the area of the base is 144 sq. in., height 29 in., and there was a little sluggishness of the steelyard and a reaction about equal to twice the weight of the table. In the case of table 4 (the stool), whose surface area is 175 sq. in., base area 64 sq. in., height 11¼ in., there was very pronounced sluggishness of the steelyard and a reaction of about 11 times the weight of the table.

In the case of the stool the obvious stiffness of the steelyard showed that there was friction somewhere during levitation. Accordingly I carefully examined the balancing mechanism of the machine, and I have come to the conclusion that the temporary want of sensitiveness was due to a twist having been applied by the operators to the platform during the experiment. It is to be noted, as mentioned above, that immediately levitation was over, the machine was perfectly sensitive again. From this consideration I am obliged to think that a large part of the reaction as measured on the machine in the case of the stool was fictitious, and represents the effects of friction on the mechanism due to the twist, or to the reaction pressure being applied other than vertically to the platform, and that in the case of table 3 some of the reaction is due to the same cause.

I will show later that during an abnormal levitation, i.e. one affected from a higher surface than the floor level (which I call a normal one), there is usually a horizontal component of the reaction acting on the platform straight outwards from the medium. This component would push the platform over on its fulcra and cause friction.

It remains to conjecture why with the stool there should be such pronounced evidence of twist or oblique reaction on the platform, and none in the case of the large séance-table. After much consideration of the phenomenon, I have come to the conclusion that levitation of a table over a raised platform is much more difficult than over a level wooden floor. There seems to be a normal levitating level with reference to the position of medium. Any alteration in this normal relation of medium and table, such as putting the table on a raised platform, increases the inherent difficulty of the phenomenon. I think also that we have some slight evidence in the friction noticeable in the case of the stool that something in the nature of a "structure" is being used. The preliminary increases of weight registered during the beginning of levitation would also suggest this.

As already mentioned, I have satisfied myself that in the general case of levitation over the floor there is no back pressure or reaction upon the floor. It is to be noted that in levitation over the platform of the weighing-machine, whose surface is some 7 in. above the floor, the smallest reaction was equal to the weight of the table, and the largest was much greater. In experiments which I shall describe later I shall hope to give a reason for this apparently anomalous condition of things.

CHAPTER VII

EXPERIMENTS WITH COMPRESSION SPRING
BALANCE UNDERNEATH THE LEVITATED TABLE

Owing to the results of experiments in which levitation was effected over the platform of a weighing-machine not proving decisive, due to what appeared to be oblique reaction forces exerted on the platform causing twist and friction of the mechanism, I thought I would place an ordinary compression balance below the table and see what would happen during levitation, if indeed the phenomenon were possible with the balance there at all. I thought of using such a balance because only the vertical component of any reaction could be registered on it, and the machine was not delicate enough to be much affected by small horizontal components, assuming that such were present. The whole thing was merely guesswork, and I am sure I was as surprised as anybody when I found it came off successfully, and not only came off but gave exceedingly valuable results. In the experiments I am now going to describe there will be a certain amount of repetition, but as I have already said, such repetition in psychic research is valuable and indeed necessary, for opportunities of obtaining similar results are very limited, and every observation that shows the least trace of value should therefore be strictly preserved. Moreover, I only arrived at the proper capacity of balance required, and the best conditions for carrying out the experiments, by a system of trial and error; but during all these preliminary tests many results of much importance, not in the direct line of the main purpose of the experiments, were obtained.

Experiment 44: A spring compression balance being placed below the table, to see if the table could be levitated without reaction on the balance.

The table was the séance one, weighing 10⅜ lb. The balance used was of the type employed in many households for weighing groceries. It had a circular dial registering up to 14 lb. by means of a pointer, and the material to be weighed was placed in a circular metal pan on top, the diameter of the pan being 9½ in. The total height of the balance (illustrated in fig. 11) was 13 in. when there was no weight in the pan.

Before elevation, the balance was placed on the floor as nearly under the centre of the table as could be judged by the eye. Fig 12 indicates the relative positions and dimensions.

Figure 11

The plan of the surface of the table is shown by the full lines, the position of the legs by the crosses, and the pan of the compression balance by the circle. My position is indicated by the letter A, immediately in front of the table and on the side remote from the medium. There was a clear space of at least 15 in. between the top of the balance and the under surface of the table. I asked the operators to levitate the table immediately above the balance.

I placed my finger on the pointer whose movement registers the weights in the pan of the balance, and awaited events. Some minutes elapsed, and then the table gave a few heaves at either end. It finally levitated a few inches from the floor, and, after remaining in the air some seconds, dropped. Some minutes passed before the levitation was again successful, and there was a lot of preliminary jerking before it was accomplished, and, as on the previous occasion, it only lasted for the briefest of periods. But during each of these evidently difficult levitations there was *no pressure on the balance beneath the table*, for the pointer remained stationary in its zero position. Thus the operators had accomplished what was required of them, but apparently only after much trouble.

Conclusion: The table may be levitated and no reaction pressure be put on the pan of the balance, but such a levitation seems difficult and not in accordance with the usual method.

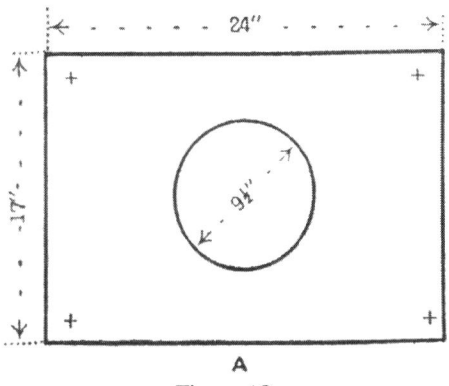

Figure 12

In thinking over the result it occurred to me that the operators were making use of that part of the surface underneath the table outside a circle projected upwards from the pan of the balance, and that this was not their normal method of levitation. On inquiring if this was the case, they replied by raps in the affirmative.

Experiment 45: The operators were told not to take any notice of the balance, but to levitate in their normal manner. To find the vertical reaction.

The séance-table and the 14 lb. Balance were used.

I placed a piece of dark cloth on the pan of the balance, as experience has shown that reflected rays from any surface upon which psychic force is exerted interfere with the ease and intensity of the phenomena. My finger was pressing lightly on the pointer on the dial of the balance, and in a very few seconds I felt the pointer moving round the dial. It moved completely round at a fairly uniform speed and clicked against the stop, the time occupied being about three seconds. Almost immediately with the completed revolution of the pointer the table rose into the air, swaying slightly backwards and forwards, the pointer remaining all the time against the stop. After some time the table suddenly dropped, and synchronously the pointer flew back round the dial to its normal zero position, nearly catching my finger in the process and nipping it between the pointer and the face of the dial. The maximum reading of the balance was 14 lb., and in order to reach the stop the pointer would have to travel a further distance equivalent to about ½ lb., so that while levitation was in progress there was a direct downward force upon the pan of the balance of at least 14½ lb.; how much more than the 14½ lb. might have been registered if the balance had had the capacity to record it, I was unable to say. I did not think, however, that it would have been very much more, as the table seemed to spring up into the air almost immediately after the completion of the revolution of the pointer round the dial. The levitation in this case was strikingly easier than that recorded in Experiment 44. The operators said it was their normal method, and there can be little doubt it is so, at least approximately, because the levitations (there were several of them) were apparently all fairly easy. The degree of difficulty seemed little more than with ordinary levitation without apparatus under the table, the only difference, so far as I could see, lying in the fact that the steadiness was not so pronounced, there being a swaying action during suspension of a character I had not noticed in the ordinary case. I think this swaying action is due to the table being supported on an area of under surface about equal to the area of the pan of the balance, whereas in the ordinary case the supporting force is somewhat more uniform over the surface.

I have said that the pointer took about three or four seconds to get round the dial while levitation was occurring. I examined the phenomenon many times during a period of about a quarter of an hour, and always found that, if the balance was approximately central with respect to the table, the levitation was almost invariably good and the speed of the pointer round the dial was always about the same; so much so, in fact, was this the case, that I had time to call out that a levitation was about to occur, well before it did occur. It is to be noted that when the pointer completed the circuit and became fast on the stop, the table appeared to spring into the air; that is the only word for it. The important fact is here brought out that the psychic force producing levitation is not applied instantly, but requires an appreciable time (about three to four seconds in this case) to reach the maximum required for levitation.

Conclusions: (1) As the weight of the table was $10\frac{3}{8}$ lb., and as the vertical reaction during levitation was always greater than $14\frac{1}{2}$ lb., it does not seem likely that there is any kind of direct stress across anything resembling a fluidic field, unless the weight of the field itself is a considerable factor.

(2) The psychic force producing levitation, judging from the augmentation of reaction, is applied gradually.

(3) At the correct instant the table seems to spring into the air.

(4) The table sways slightly when levitated above the pan of the balance.

(5) The levitating force can be removed instantly.

Experiment 46: Two legs of the table remaining on the floor, the other two rise in the air and move up and down. To find the effect on spring balance placed underneath the table.

The ordinary séance-table and 14 lb. balance were used.

The raised end of the table was jerking quickly up and down in the air. The pointer of the compression balance under the table moved quickly to and fro over the dial in correspondence with the movements of the raised end, the maximum reading being about 7 lb. and the range being about 3 lb.

On another occasion of partial levitation with the same jerking motion the balance *was not affected at all*, which would seem to show that in that case the psychic force was applied somewhere outside the projection from pan to under surface of table.

During the series of levitations with the 14 lb. compression balance below the table, several points were noticed which I put down under letter headings:—

(A) On two occasions of good levitation the pointer of the balance remained steady for the duration of levitation at about 12 lb. instead of going up against the stop and remaining hard pressed against it. This may have been due to the whole of the reaction not being upon the pan of the balance.

(B) With the table *steadily* tilted on two legs, the pointer on several trials indicated a downward force of about 7 lb.

(C) Sometimes if there was a hitch in the levitation the pointer would gradually move round to 7 lb. or 8 lb., the table either not rising at all, or tilting just a little, and then the pointer would fly back to zero. The operators would then try again for complete levitation, usually successfully.

(D) I asked on one occasion that the operators should lower the table gently and remove the psychic force gradually, instead of suddenly, as was usually done. The result was that the table descended to the floor slowly, and then the pointer of the balance moved slowly and uniformly back round the dial to zero, taking about six seconds in the process.

(E) When the table was levitated and the pointer against the stop at 14½ lb., I placed my hand and part of my arm in the scale-pan of the balance. I felt no pressure at all, and both the levitation and the reaction were un-affected.

(F) I grasped the near edge of the scale-pan, and felt it moving down while the table was being levitated and moving up when the psychic force was being removed.

Experiment 47: This is, strictly speaking, a series of experiments, similar in the main to Experiments 45 and 46, but with this difference, that a compression balance reading up to 28 lb. was used in place of the one whose maximum reading was 14 lb. In the previous experiments the capacity of the balance was too small to enable the maximum reading to be obtained when the table was levitated, although it was large enough to allow of many interesting points being noted. Therefore, on this occasion I brought to the séance room a balance which read to 28 lb., and I expected that this would be quite large enough to measure the vertical reaction. There was no substantial difference in size or shape of the two balances. During a series of levitations, using this new balance, I found that all the results I have mentioned in Experiments 45 and 46 (with the exception of (A), Experiment 46) were completely verified. There was one important misconception, however. When actual levitation occurred, the pointer on the balance did not read a few pounds over 14, as I thought it would, but actually went round the scale and on to the stop, and only just when at the stop were there signs that levitation was imminent. I was much surprised, because I felt almost certain that the vertical reaction was not much greater than 14 lb. However, there was no doubt about the matter, for during four or five levitations the same thing occurred. It would appear that this balance was just on the small side for registering the levitation reaction.

Conclusion: The vertical reaction for the séance-table, weighing 10 lb., is greater than 28 lb., though probably only a little greater.

I had noticed what I thought was a pushing force on the body of the balance during levitation from the direction of the medium. To see if there was in reality a horizontal pushing force as well as a vertical force, I carried out the following experiment.

Experiment 48: To find the horizontal component of the reaction.

The apparatus employed is that shown diagrammatically in fig. 13.

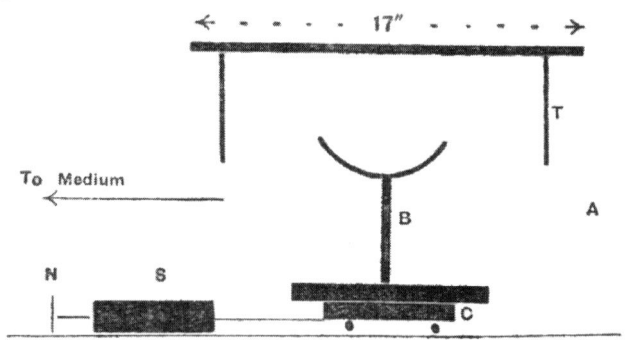

Figure 13

B is the compression balance (reading to 14 lb.) placed on top of an iron carriage C, which runs on ball bearings, and which is so free from friction that a force of $\frac{1}{10}$ lb. suffices to pull it along the floor. N is a nail driven into the floor. S is an ordinary Salter tension spring balance reading to 20 lb., tied to the nail N and to the carriage C. T is the levitated table. Between A and N is my approximate position of observation.

I placed a finger of the right hand on the pointer of the tension balance S, and a finger of the left hand on the pointer of the compression balance B. I then asked the operators to levitate the table, when in the usual way the pointer on B gradually moved round to 14½ lb. against the stop, and then the table sprang up into the air. The pointer on the tension balance also simultaneously moved along the scale, and the average of half a dozen levitations gave for it a rough value of about 4 lb. To confirm roughly this reading, I pushed backwards on the compression balance B, and distinctly felt a force of about that magnitude pushing against me.

That the horizontal pushing force on the balance B is not an independent force may be inferred from the following:— Several times during levitation strong upward jerks of the table were given. On all such occasions the pointer on the tension balance S indicated a sudden increase of a pound or two, and when the jerking motion was completed it went back to the normal reading of about 4 lb. steady pull.

Conclusion: The horizontal component of the reaction when the séance-table of weight 10⅜ lb. is levitated above the 14 lb. balance is apparently about 4 lb.; and this component acts directly outwards from the medium.

At a later date I made a further experiment with the object of determining accurately the horizontal component of the reaction.

Experiment 49: To endeavour to determine accurately the horizontal component of the reaction.

I rigged up the apparatus as shown in fig. 13. The balances were, however, different. The compression balance was the one reading to 28 lb. (not 14 lb.), although its over-all dimensions were about the same; and the tension balance was a much larger one, with larger scale divisions than that used in the previous experiment. It was new, and read up to 20 lb.

During the course of this experiment I proved to my satisfaction that the horizontal and vertical forces are only components of a single force. In three or four cases, with a finger of one hand on the tension pointer and a finger of the other on the compression pointer, I felt the absolutely synchronous and proportionate movements of the two: when a hitch in the levitation occurred, the tension pointer stopped (or very nearly stopped), the compression pointer being against the stop; they started simultaneously, and I could tell when a levitation was about to occur by the forward movement of the tension pointer just as well as by that of the compression pointer.

The correct values of the pushing force from medium when the table is steadily levitated above the 28 lb. balance is 5¼ lb., and this is certainly correct within ¼ lb. (I followed up the movement of the pointer by a piece of chalk behind it, and this left a sharp straight mark on the scale.) This value of 5¼ lb. is the result of many careful readings. A value of about 4 lb. was obtained in experiment 48, but the spring balance used in that test was not so accurate as that employed in the present one; also, the two compression balances, although very much alike, varied a little in height and other particulars; and again, there may be special reasons why on different evenings the horizontal component of the reaction should vary a little, even though all the apparatus, and its disposition with reference to the medium, remained constant.

Experiment 50: To find the exact value of the vertical downward force on the pan of the balance while the séance-table, weight 10⅜ lb., was steadily levitated above it.

The 14 lb. and 28 lb. balances being both insufficient to measure the vertical reaction under the levitated séance-table, it was necessary to employ a balance having a still larger capacity. Accordingly, I next chose for this purpose what is known as a parcel balance, because, as its name implies, it is used for weighing parcels. Its maximum reading was 56 lb., and instead of having as circular scale-pan it had a flat weighing surface of rectangular planished steel 14 in. × 9 in. Its height from base to top, unloaded, was 13½ in. A photograph of it in connection with other apparatus is given in fig. 17.

Fig. 15 shows the plan of the séance-table and pan of balance. The final experiments with this balance were made in conjunction with those for evaluating the horizontal component of the reaction (see Experiments 48 and 49 and fig. 13).

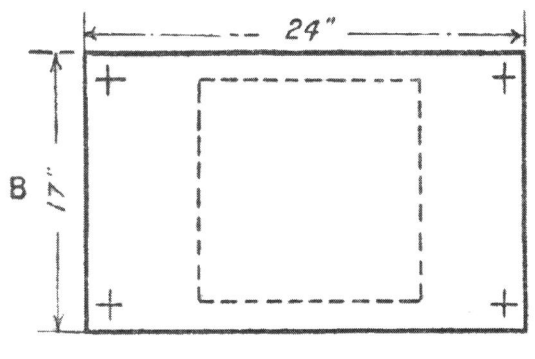

Figure 15

The parcel balance was placed on top of the little frictionless carriage C, immediately under the table. The total height of pan of balance from floor was then about 15½ in. First of all I sat *outside* the circle and asked for levitation, which after a time was given. An interesting feature of this levitation was the audible click of the mechanism of both tension and compression balances as they took up their loads. Having therefore seen that the operators could produce the phenomenon under the difficult circumstances named, i.e. with a large balance under the table and a tension balance near medium (see fig.

13), I entered the circle and placed myself at the position, with reference to the table, of the letter B (fig. 15), and not A as in Experiment 44, fig. 12, the reason being that the pan of the parcel balance was so large that it was more convenient to put it under the table, so that the dial was facing at right angles to the medium and not directly opposite her. I put the piece of black cloth over the pan and my finger on the pointer of the balance. I had also a piece of chalk for marking the pointer position. I asked for levitation, but, contrary to custom, did not get it. It would seem that my entering the circle had interfered in some way with its psychic equilibrium; and although the operators tried hard and often, as was evidenced by the pointer travelling a good way round the dial, they did not actually succeed in securing a levitation. I suggested to them that I should lower the balance a little, and asked them if that would help. They answered, "Yes." So I took the balance off the carriage and placed it on the floor, which reduced its total height about 2 in. This was immediately efficacious, and levitation soon occurred. I took the value of the downward force on the pan for about half a dozen steady levitations.

Result: The vertical downward force on pan is 30 lb., and this value is correct to 1½ lb. either way, and probably correct to ½ lb. either way.

The machine was tested for accuracy before the experiment.

The reader must not think that the obtaining of the above result—on which I place much importance—was an easy matter. Because of the size of the balance beneath the table it was difficult, and called for much patience and accuracy on the part of the operators. About four séance hours were occupied altogether in obtaining it and in verifying and reverifying it on different evenings.

Conclusion:
Weight of table .... =   10⅜ lb.

COMPRESSION SPRING BALANCE

Vertical downward force on compression balance during steady levitation..= 30 lb.
Horizontal pushing force on balance during steady levitation ....= 5¼ lb.

The next thing I wished to find out was whether there was a quantitative relation between the height above the floor of the platform from which levitation was effected and the vertical downward reaction on the platform.

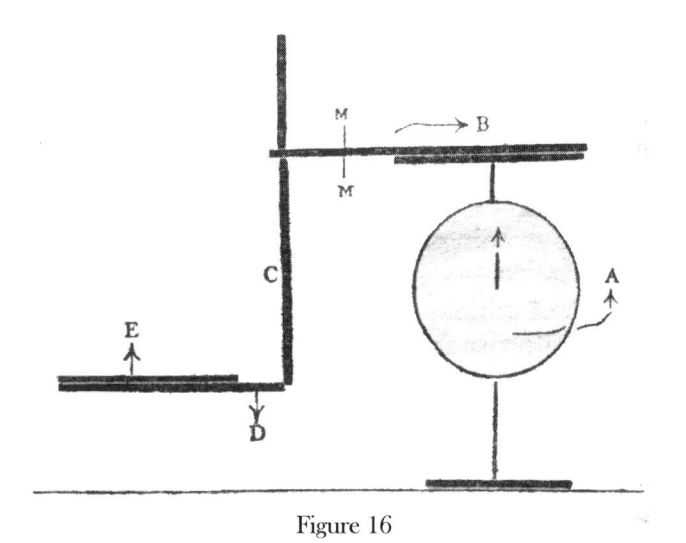

Figure 16

Experiment 51: To find the relation between height of platform and vertical downward reaction during levitation.

Fig. 16 gives a diagrammatic sketch of the apparatus employed, whilst a photograph is also shown (fig. 17).

A is the parcel spring balance (see Experiment 50) reading up to 56 lb., with a flat rectangular planished steel pan 14 in. × 9 in.

B is a flat iron bar clamped firmly to the pan of the balance C is a circular iron rod which can slide up and down through a hole in the end of B, and which can be fixed to B by a pin arrangement at intervals in height of 2 in.

D is a flat iron bar fixed at right angles to C.

E is a flat rectangular-shaped piece of wood fixed to the top of D

Figure 17

The method of carrying out the experiment was as follows:— The apparatus was placed on the floor, to which the base of the balance was tightly clamped in order to prevent motion as the psychic reaction was exerted on E. The table was then placed on the floor centrally over the rectangular wooden surface E, with the consequence that the edge of the table came to about the line MM, all that part of the apparatus to the left of MM being below the table. The idea was that the reaction would be exerted on the flat surface E; and as E could be gradually raised, the various reactions for the different heights could be read on the balance A.

COMPRESSION SPRING BALANCE

Needless to say, the whole apparatus was made exceedingly rigid, and, in spite of the large overhang, when tested in the laboratory was found to be practically accurate.

This experiment is so important, and the chance of performing it occurs so seldom, that I will not apologise for going somewhat minutely into details. In the first test, the rectangular piece of wood E was ordinary soft wood, and measured 12 in. × 9 in. It was fixed to the flat iron bar D by two ordinary screws through holes in D. The apparatus was placed under the table so that the lower surface of D just cleared the floor. I kept my finger firmly on the pointer of the balance A. Levitation was then asked for and obtained. When I was sure of the result for this position, I raised the platform E 2 in. by sliding C up through the hole in the end of B and fixing C in the new position by the pin arrangement provided. Then I obtained levitation for this position. Then the platform was raised another 2 in., and the experiment proceeded as before. I always took care that E was practically centrally under the table. I usually, for each position, took about three levitations to ensure accuracy. The following is the result of the first experiment. Heights may be considered accurate to ½ in.

Weight of table .... = 10⅜ lb.
Dimensions of platform E .... = 12 in. × 9 in.
Initial no-load reading on balance
due to weight of apparatus .... = 8¾ lb.

Height of platform from floor (in inches)	Net vertical reaction on platform during levitation (in lbs.).
1½	0
3½	½
5½	3
7½	23¼

During one of the last tests at the height of 7½ in., the operators evidently applied the psychic pressure a little off the centre of the platform, for the two screws which held it in position on the flat iron bar D were wrenched out of the wood. Accordingly, further tests could not be proceeded with that evening.

For the next series of tests I substituted for the soft wood a piece of 5 ply wood, and for the screws a couple of ¼ in. bolts.

Experiment 52: Second experiment to find the quantitative relation between height of platform and vertical reaction. *Time*: some weeks later than the date of Experiment 51.

Before I carried out the second experiment I made a slight alteration on the séance-table, which affected its weight a little. Up to that time the table had possessed two light wooden bars across its width at either end near the floor, their object being, of course, to add rigidity to the legs. In order to show that these were not essential to levitation I had them sawn off.

Weight of table .... = 10 lb.
Dimensions of platform (see fig 16) .... = 12 in. × 9 in.
Initial no-load reading on balance
due to weight of apparatus .... = 9 lb.

Height of platform from which levitation is effected (in inches)	Net vertical reaction on platform during levitation (in pounds)	
	Test A	Test B
1	0	0
3	¾	¾
5	22	26
7	27	31
9	34½	33
11	36½	38

The method of carrying out the two tests A and B was as follows:— I first did test A, commencing with the platform at its nearest distance to the floor and taking either two or three levitations for each height, so as to obtain the results as accurately as possible. When I had worked through all the heights in this way, I went right through them again from bottom to top (test B). It will be observed that there is a variation of a few pounds in some of the heavier readings between the two sets.

During the course of the séance, over twenty separate levitations were given by the operators.

I wish to emphasise a particular point with regard to this experiment—a point which I think will eventually prove to be of great importance in the elucidation of the mystery of psychic force. It is this: At the greater heights—those in which the reactions are heavy—the downward vertical force on the platform did not become steady (as might have been expected) as soon as levitation was effected. On the contrary, the force in all cases continued to increase for a couple of seconds or so after levitation. From 5 lb. to 8 lb. is my estimate of the amount of downward force *added after levitation was complete,* and before the pointer on the balance ceased moving, which it, however, eventually did in all cases. The readings given above represent the final steady values.

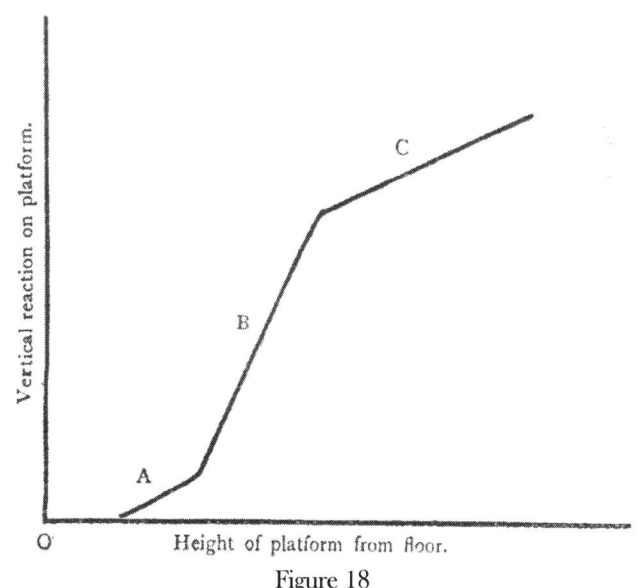

Figure 18

And now a word or two on the interpretation of the results of Experiments 51 and 52. The three tests, although they do not give identical results for the different heights, are, however, fairly consistent. They all show—

(1) That on the floor, and for two or three inches above it, there is no reaction (thus verifying the results of Experiment 38).

(2) A very slight reaction is just noticeable at a height of three inches from the floor.

(3) The reaction in all three cases suddenly increases. For instance, in Experiment 51, from inch 5½ to inch 7½, it changes from 3 lb. to 23¼ lb.; in Experiment 52, test A, from inch 3 to inch 5, it changes from ¾ lb. to 22 lb.; in test B, from inch 3 to inch 5, from ¾ lb. to 26 lb.

(4) After the sudden increase of reaction pressure referred to in (3), the rate of increase of pressure with height greatly diminishes.

The graph, fig. 18, shows roughly how the reaction varies. There seems first to be a gradual rise of pressure (A), then a sudden rise (B), and then a slower and fairly uniform increase (C).

Experiment 53: To find the vertical component of the reaction when a small stool is levitated immediately above a compression balance.

I placed the drawing-board (covered with a piece of rough dark carpet) on top of the 56 lb, parcel balance (see Experiment 50), and the stool (table 4) on top of the board, and asked for levitation.

Fig. 19 indicates the arrangement. This levitation was evidently a most difficult one for the operators; in fact, I think it was the most difficult one I have come across, not even excepting that of the séance table over the platform of the weighing-machine (see Experiment 41). It was attempted at least a dozen times before being finally successful. What usually happened was that the pointer on the balance would move round to 20 lb. or so, and then, just when levitation was evidently about to occur, the little stool would topple over, when I would have to place it upright again. It seemed to me that something was trying to get under the stool, but, owing to the small amount of space available, and to the height of the platform, was unsuccessful. At length, however, just when I was about to give up the experiment, even in spite of the desire of the operators, who told me by raps to hold on, the stool went up about 8 in. into the air and remained there quite steady for from 8 to 10 seconds. Two such levitations gave for the vertical downward force on the balance 24 lb., and two others gave 24½ lb. The weight of the board (with carpet) was 5½ lb., so that the vertical downward force on the balance while the stool was steadily levitated was 24¼ (the average) 5½ = 18¾ lb., or 6.8 times the weight of the stool.

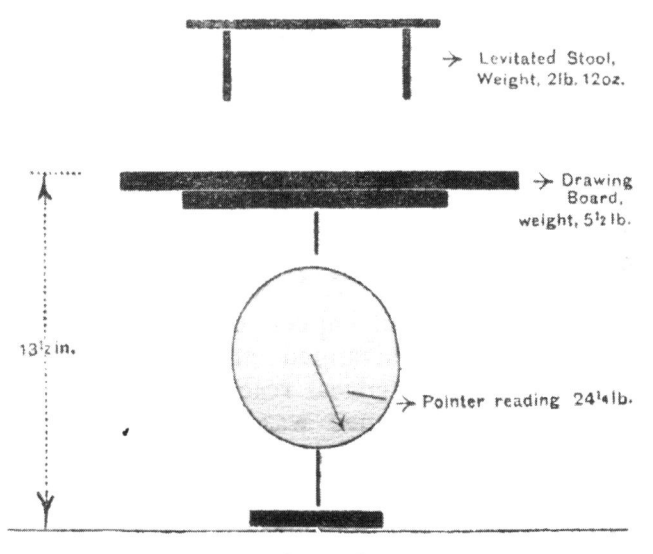

Figure 19

In order to make sure that this value of 18¾ lb. was not fictitious, during several of the unsuccessful attempts at levitation referred to above I grasped the edge of the drawing-board and lifted it a little. I found, as anticipated, that my estimate of the downward force on the board agreed roughly with the reading on the balance.

Experiment 54: The work done in the previous tests gave me a fairly accurate idea as to what was happening below the table. In order to see if I could deduce what exactly would happen under certain conditions, I arranged an experiment in which the vertical reaction on the compression balance was indicated by the ringing of an electric bell.

Apparatus:

(a) The séance-table, weight 10 lb.

(b) A compression balance reading to 28 lb.

(c) An electric bell and battery with about 20 ft. of insulated wire.

(d) A paper-clip made of metal, such as is used to hold numbers of sheets of paper together.

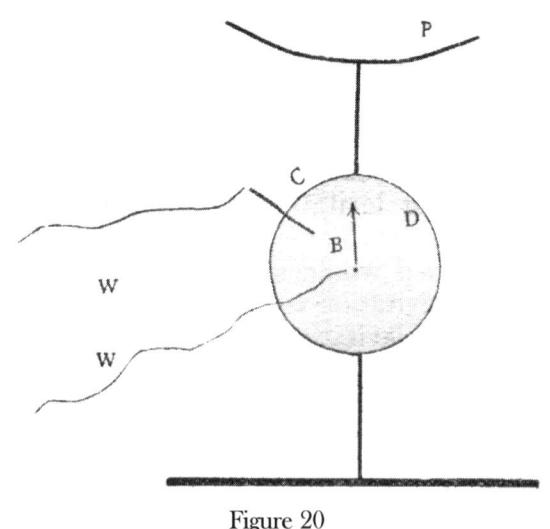

Figure 20

Method: I took the little weighing-machine or balance, and, having scraped the insulation off the end of one of the electric-bell wires, attached the wire to the pointer of the balance. This was done by taking out the screw at the centre, twisting the end of the wire round it, and then screwing it back securely in place. The end of the other electric-bell wire was fastened securely to the paper-clip. The clip itself was fixed over the edge of the dial, and was insulated from it by pieces of brown paper being placed between it and the surface of the dial.

In fig. 20, P is the pan of the balance, D the dial, B the pointer, W W the wires going to the electric bell, and C the clip. The clip was fixed about the 20 lb. mark on the dial. The idea of the whole thing was that when the pointer should turn round sufficiently to come into contact with the clip, electric contact would be made and the bell would ring. With the séance-table of weight 10 lb., the actual vertical reaction was greater than 20 lb. (see Experiment 50), but I set the clip at 20 lb. so as to make sure of good mechanical contact.

I placed the balance on the floor centrally under the table, and the bell and battery on the mantelpiece, letting the wires run along the floor. There was a clear space of at least 15 in. between pan of balance and under surface of table. I placed a piece of rough dark cloth on the pan. I expected to find the following results during levitation of the table over the balance:—

(1) The bell would start ringing a second or two before levitation actually took place.

(2) During levitation the bell would probably ring continuously.

(3) The varying height of the levitation would probably make no difference to the ringing of the bell.

As a matter of fact, when levitation was in progress the above three results were exactly what were obtained.

I recommend an experimenter, if he has a levitating medium at hand, to carry out this experiment. It is simple and also effective, for the observer can take a stroll round the circle while it is going on, can see the table levitated, can hear the bell ringing, and can see that all hands are held in chain order and that feet are on the floor. He can also ask the members of the circle to hold their hands up to the level of their heads, and make other tests that occur to him.

Experiment 55: To discover what would happen when, the medium having been placed on weighing-machine, and a compression balance having been placed under the table, the table levitated.

Fig. 21 shows the arrangement. M is the medium seated on the weighing-machine, T is the levitated table, and B is the compression balance.

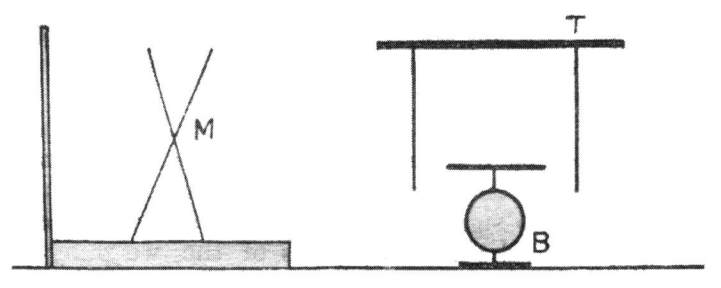

Figure 21

I first of all balanced exactly the weight of medium, chair, and drawing board (it was 9 st. 10 lb. 12 oz.), and allowed the steelyard to rest lightly on the bottom stop. Then I placed the 14 lb. compression balance (see Experiment 44) under the table and asked for levitation. I kept my finger tightly on the pointer of the balance. Unfortunately, this experiment is in no wise complete, and I never had an opportunity of repeating it (though I may hope for one in the future), and the result obtained, while accurate so far as it goes, is not exact as regards figures. During levitation the pointer of the compression balance was hard up against the stop. I asked the operators to drop the table suddenly, which they did, and the pointer on the compression balance immediately flew back round the dial to zero. Four seconds afterwards the click of the steelyard of the weighing-machine was heard as it fell on the bottom stop; that is to say, while the table was levitated there was a vertical reaction on the compression balance, and also an increased weight on the medium.

The four seconds was the computation from three similar tests, and was made by me and also by an independent observer. This time lag has, I think, no significance, being due solely to the inertia of the moving parts of the weighing-machine.

How much extra weight was on the medium while the table was in the air above the balance I am unable to say; probably, as I shall show later on, not an amount equal to the weight of the table.

Experiment 56: Crackling sound in the wood of surface of table during levitation.

During one of the tests mentioned in this chapter, I heard a sort of crackling sound in the wood of the under surface of the table just when levitation was commencing, as though the fibres were being subjected to stress—to a stress which was pushing them apart from one another, as it were. I have only heard this particular kind of sound on two occasions.

Experiment 57: Thud under table at commencement of levitation.

During one of the levitations I heard a soft thud under the centre of the top of the table as if a column of some softish substance had been pushed on it. I remarked on this to the members of the circle, and on the very next levitation I again heard the same light thud. It would seem that the operators had heard what I had said and had repeated the performance for my benefit. These were the only occasions on which I ever heard the noise. Possibly it was the impact of the levitating force delivered a little more heavily than usual.

CHAPTER VIII

COMPLETION OF THE EXPERIMENTS ON LEVITATION

Experiment 58: The effect of placing a charged electroscope under the levitated table.

I took an electroscope of the disc type, charged it, and placed it nearly centrally under the steadily levitated table, allowing it to remain there for about half a minute. Result: no effect on the electroscope, the leaves remaining as far apart as before.

The investigation of the space between the medium and the levitated table is a most important matter. Unfortunately, this region is a most difficult place in which to experiment, for the placing of apparatus within it, or rather within the vital part of it, immediately breaks down the line of communication; and as this line, or these lines, seem difficult to form, and once broken cause the cessation of phenomena for quite a long period of time, the experimenter has to be careful what he is doing. Also the unscientific meddling with this part of space is apt to be physically injurious to the medium.

Experiment 59: Investigation of the space between the medium and the table jerking about the floor.

Apparatus: I had constructed a very delicate electric contact, consisting of two pieces of flat clock spring, separated from each other by a distance of about ⅛ in. A piece of light cardboard about 3 in. × 3½ in. was hinged at its top end to a flat piece of wood, and rested on the top spring. The contact was placed in an electric-bell circuit, and it was so adjusted that breathing upon it strongly was sufficient to make the bell ring.

In fig. 22, W is the flat piece of wood; C the piece of cardboard hinged at A; S S the two pieces of flat spring the coming into contact of which rang the electric bell (not shown).

The table was jerking about on the floor. I moved the contact-maker here and there in the air in front of the medium, keeping the surface of the cardboard nearest to her and roughly parallel to her body and perpendicular to any stress line likely to come from her. At a certain spot about 2 ft. above the floor the bell rang, and simultaneously the table stopped its movement along the floor.

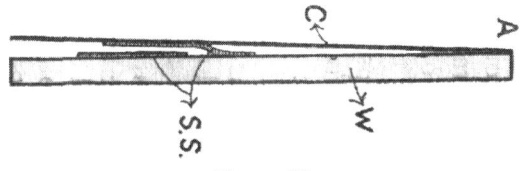

Figure 22

Experiment 60: Investigation of space between medium and levitated table.

Apparatus: Same as in Experiment 59.

I asked for levitation of the séance-table, and while it was in progress I moved the contact-maker about in front of the medium as in the previous test. At practically the same spot the bell rang again and *the table instantly dropped.* The operators would not allow me to proceed with the experiment. They affirmed, by means of raps, that the contact-maker was in the stress-line from medium to table.

Experiments 59 and 60 show two things very plainly; (1) that the contact-maker was cutting across a link connecting medium to table, and (2) along this link there was mechanical pressure *from medium to table.*

I append some remarks I made in *Light* when describing the above Experiments:—

"I have some reason to believe that the establishing of these stress-lines (the links) is for the operators a difficult process, and that once formed they remain more or less *in situ* for the duration of the séance. I think they may be linked to tunnels somewhat laboriously cut through resisting material. Their basis seems to be physical, for I have actually felt the motion of material particles near the ankles (and proceeding outwards from them) of the medium (the stress-lines seem to commence sometimes at the wrists and ankles of my medium), and I have noticed during the rapping that when my hand interferes with the particle flow—which seems to correspond with a stress-line—the rapping has ceased for quite a long time and could seemingly only be restarted with difficulty. In other words, the path had been obliterated. I do not think the particles of matter (for such I am assuming them to be) are the cause of the pressure which lifts the table. I think they are the connecting links which allow the psychic pressure to be transmitted, much in the manner that a wire is the path which enables electricity to flow."

Experiment 61: Reaction on the floor below levitated table.

To verify the results of previous experiments which showed that when the séance-table was levitated above the floor there was no reaction on the floor, I took advantage of the delicate contact-maker used in Experiment 59. Having placed it on the floor under the table, I asked for levitation. During the preliminary jerkings, etc., and also during levitation, the bell did *not* ring—showing, as was expected, that there was no pressure on the floor.

Experiment 62: Condition of the medium during levitation.

During many of the levitations mentioned in the previous experiments I examined the medium. Her arms, whether held by the sitters on either side of her, or resting on her knees, were always stiff, i.e. he muscles seemed to be under great stress, making the arms even sometimes iron-like in their rigidity. Especially was this rigidity noticeable at the bend of the arm, though right from shoulder to wrist the amount of the muscular tension was surprising. While the stool was steadily levitated at the abnormal height of 4 feet, her arms were excessively stiff, even stiffer than when the séance-table, nearly four times as heavy, was suspended. The medium herself says that high levitations affect her muscular system most. She says the muscular rigidity is not confined to her arms but occurs all over her body, although not to the same extent.

Of late months I am inclined to think that a change has been occurring. I do not think her arms are at present so rigid during levitation as they once were. Perhaps this is due to the reaction upon her becoming more diffused.

Experiment 63: Possible weight of structure used to levitate the table.

I said to the operators, "I wish you to put the 'power' you use for levitating the table under the table, but not to levitate it or act on it in any way." I repeated the request slowly several times. They said they thoroughly understood what I required. I had previously balanced the weight of medium (Who was sitting on the weighing-machine), chair, and drawing-board (see Experiments in chapter III). The combined weight was 9 st. 10 lb. 12 oz. I watched the machine carefully. The medium's weight began to decrease, slowly and a little spasmodically, and it became fairly steady again at 8 st. 10 lb., though there were fluxes below this. Hence, according to the operators, the weight of the field or structure required for levitation of the séance-table was about 14 lb. or 15 lb. But as they may have been doubtful of my meaning—though they did not appear to be so,—I do not propose to pay much attention to this result.

Experiment 64: Evidence of some sort or preparation on the part of the operators just previous to levitation.

The observing of many levitation experiments has shown me that the operators have to make a preparation for the phenomenon. The following test, which has occurred often, will enable the reader to understand what I mean. The pan of the 28 lb. compression balance (used in some of the experiments already described) was not fixed tightly on the stem of the balance, but was a loose fit upon it.

In fig. 23 the pan P is shown fitting loosely over the circular socket A, from which it can be removed by simply raising it up. The consequence of the loose fit is that if the pan is lightly shaken it rattles. When I placed this balance below the table and asked for levitation, what usually happened was that from half a minute to a minute before levitation the pan would rattle, although of course no one was touching it. On these occasions no pressure was registered on the balance. So regularly was this the case with levitation over this particular balance, that I had to come to the conclusion that what was happening was that the operators were laying some kind of a line, structure, substratum—call it what you will—from the medium to the pan of the balance, and that this was an essential and necessary preliminary to the accomplishment of the phenomenon.

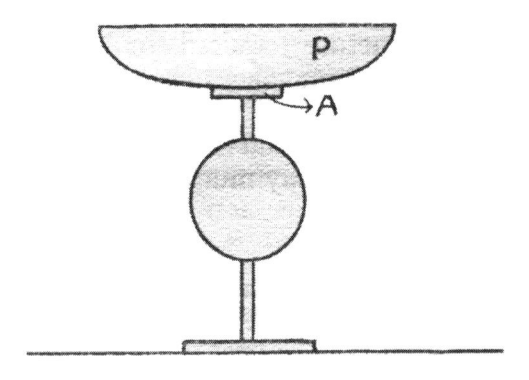

Figure 23

The following notes are taken from one of my articles in *Light* on this same matter, and deal in a general way with other balances than the one mentioned above—i.e. balances in which the pan was rigidly fixed:—

"Suppose I am working at compression-balance experiments below the table. At the conclusion of each test I usually bring a fairly strong light right into the centre of the circle, in order thoroughly to examine instruments and so on. When I do this, the next levitation required does not commence at once, but may take a few minutes. Before it commences I become conscious that *preparations are being made for it*, by a kind of shock being given to the apparatus, a shock which does not produce pressure. Perhaps a quarter or half a minute later levitation occurs. It would seem that a line was being made, so to speak, and that the phenomenon could not ensue until it was properly in position. Witness the thud of the supposed column, well before levitation (see Experiment 57). If I do *not* bring a white light into the circle, levitations follow one another rapidly, for the structure seems not to be disturbed and therefore does not require to be renewed or partially renewed."

Experiment 65: The presence of actual matter below the levitated table.

On one occasion, while the table was levitated (it was a difficult case of the phenomenon over a compression balance) I placed my hand under it near the top. As in previous tests, I felt no sense of pressure whatever, but I *did* feel a clammy, cold, almost oily sensation—in fact an indescribable sensation, as though the air there were mixed with particles of dead and disagreeable matter. Perhaps the best word to describe the feeling is "reptilian." I have felt the same substance often—and I think it is a substance—in the vicinity of the medium, but there it has appeared to me to be moving outwards from her. Once felt, the experimenter always recognises it again. This was the only occasion on which I have felt it under the levitated table, though perhaps it is always there, but not usually in such an intense form. Its presence under the table and also in the vicinity of the medium shows that it has something to do with the levitation; and in short I think there can be little doubt that it is actual matter temporarily taken from the medium's body and put back at the end of the séance, and that it is the basic principle underlying the transmission of psychic force.

The table soon dropped when I moved my hand to and fro in amongst this psychic stuff.

Experiment 66: To find how much weight is permanently lost by each sitter during the séance.

I took the weight of each sitter at the beginning and the end of the séance, which lasted for about an hour and a half. The following are the results:—

Names of sitters	Weight before séance	Weight after séance
Miss Kathleen Goligher (medium)	8 st. 6 lb. 6 oz.	8 st. 6 lb. 4 oz.
Mr. Goligher	8 st. 13 lb. 8 oz.	8 st. 13 lb. 8 oz.
Miss Anna Goligher	7 st. 1 lb. 4 oz.	7 st. 1 lb. 2 oz.
Miss Lily Goligher	5 st. 7 lb. 4 oz.	5 st. 7 lb. 2 oz.
Mrs Morrison	7 st. 5 lb. 12 oz.	7 st. 5 lb. 6 oz.
Mr. Morrison	9 st. 9 lb. 12 oz.	9 st. 9 lb. 11 oz.
Dr. Crawford	10 st. 9 lb. 14 oz.	10 st. 9 lb. 8 oz.

At the close of the séance, and just before the re-weighing, Mr. Morrison in a moment of forgetfulness drank half a glass of water. This was weighed and the amount subtracted from his final weight, which may, however, be an ounce or two out. One of the members of the circle, Master Sam Goligher, was absent on holiday.

More careful weighings were made. All precautions were taken that nobody should possess a handkerchief, say, at the conclusion of the sitting who did not possess it at the beginning.

It will be seen that I have included myself in the weighings, although I was not a member of the circle but was moving in and out of it all the time attending to the experimental work on hand.

When we study this result we see that there is an almost general permanent loss of weight, for, with the exception of one sitter, everybody lost a little. In no case does it amount to much more than a few ounces. It will be noted with interest that the medium lost only two ounces. The greatest sufferers seem to have been Mrs. Morrison and myself, who both lost six ounces, the maximum in any individual case.

Total weight of sitters, including myself, before séance.	Total weight of sitters, including myself, after séance.	Total loss of weight at end of séance.
57 st. 11 lb. 12 oz.	57 st. 10 lb. 9 oz.	1 lb. 3 oz.

Now, the question arises with regard to this experiment how far this permanent loss of weight of 19 oz. is due to phenomenal activities and how far to natural causes. The sitting was held on a very warm evening (temperature about 70° F.), and the room was somewhat small. There was a considerable amount of phenomena.

As to the losses of weight due to natural causes I am not able to speak. Personally, while without expert knowledge on the subject, I would not have thought there could have been such a loss by natural causes alone, even on a warm summer evening in a small room.

The next question that arises is regarding my own loss of weight. I was not a member of the circle. I was moving about the room practically all the time, in and out of the circle, attending to the experimental work on hand. Now, were the entities taking matter from me? That is, if people other than the regular sitters are in the room, altogether outside the chain of the circle, can the operators abstract matter from them for the production of psychic energy? Or is the abstraction confined to members of the circle? It looks as though the former is the case.

It is not so much a question as to whether the members of the circle are used in some way by the operating entities, as to whether matter is *permanently* extracted from the bodies of the members. That the members of the circle are of some use may easily be observed. Occasionally when I have experimented with a member short I think I have noticed that phenomena were not so powerful or prolonged. But a surer sign that the members of the circle are used is the tremendous spasmodic jerk that goes round the whole circle just previous to a difficult levitation being attempted by the operators, especially when psychic energy has been somewhat wanting and there does not seem to be any reservoir of it to draw upon, so to speak. At such a time I have asked the operators to produce levitation. In a few seconds the members would be overtaken with a severe spasmodic jerk which seemed to travel right round the circle. Then perhaps a quarter of a minute afterwards levitation would occur. I have noticed this too often to be deceived about it.

During the opening of a séance, say for the first quarter of an hour, the bodies of the sitters are usually subjected to intermittent muscular jerking. After that period of time this ceases altogether, or only takes place occasionally. It seems to me that the meeting of the process is that *something is being loosened* from the bodies of the members of the circle—a something which then circulates round the sitters either through their bodies or in space immediately surrounding their bodies.

Experiment 67: An X-ray fluorescent screen (platinocyanide of barium) placed below levitated table.

While the table was steadily levitated, I placed an X-ray fluorescent screen below it and in space surrounding it (the room was darkened for the purpose.)

Result: There was no sign of fluorescence.

CHAPTER IX

A CANTILEVER THEORY FOR LEVITATION

I propose in this chapter to bring forward a theory for levitation based chiefly on the results of the sixty-seven experiments already described.

Let us first of all consider for a little the results of experiment 50. It will be remembered that the séance-table was steadily levitated over a compression balance, and that a large vertical downward force was noted; experiment also showed that there was a pushing force from the medium. The values, as the result of much careful experimenting, were as follows:—

Weight of séance-table .... = 10⅜ lb.
Vertical downward force on compression
balance during levitation .... = 30 lb.
Horizontal pushing force from medium .... = 5¼ lb.

Besides obtaining the above values, I also took the distance of medium from table, the height of the top of her head from the floor, distance of her knees from the table, and so on. I then set out a scale diagram of her position, and the positions of table and of compression balance. The first point in the inquiry was to see if the levitation of the table could be explained by any system of two, three, or even four forces in equilibrium, taking the three known quantities enumerated above derived from experiment. The result, however, was failure. No system of simple statics will explain the phenomenon—at any rate, so far as I can see.

When I had convinced myself of this, I had to look around for another theory, and the one that seemed to me most likely was the "beam" theory, and in particular the "cantilever."

A cantilever is a beam firmly fixed at one end and free at the other.

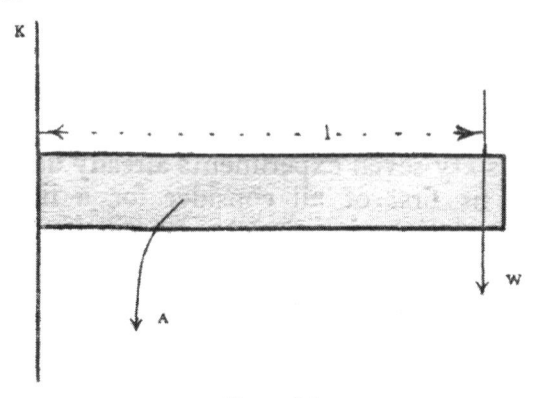

Figure 24

In fig. 24, A is the cantilever firmly built into the wall K. A weight W is shown suspended from the free end. Let us suppose the medium takes the place of the wall and that the cantilever projects from her in the manner shown, and that the table during levitation takes the place of the weight W. As to the structure of this psychic cantilever I am not at present concerned, and am only dealing with the idea that a cantilever—resembling in its qualities a rigid beam—is in reality present. I propose to see, in effect, if the theory of the cantilever explains the mechanics of the levitated table.

(1) During steady levitation above the floor with no apparatus below the table, the weight of the table is practically added to that of the medium (Experiments 2, 3, 4).

This agrees with the cantilever theory. The beam being free at the end, it is obvious that the weight added to it is in effect added to the medium.

(2) The medium is under stress. The muscles of her arms from wrist to shoulder are stiff and often iron-like in their rigidity, and other parts of her body are affected similarly, though to a less degree (Experiment 62).

At the root of the cantilever there is a shearing force W and a bending movement W1; hence we would expect to see some signs of distress on the part of the medium. The bending moment, although somewhat variable, is seldom less than 250 lb. in., if we take the psychic cantilever as fixed to the trunk of the medium.

(3) There is no reaction on the floor under the table (Experiments 38, 51, 52, 61).

This agrees with the cantilever theory. The free end being up in the air, the weight W depresses it a little, but does not affect the floor in any way. For a long time I was under the impression that some kind of psychic equilibrium was established, and that there was a reaction upon the floor, that, in fact, the readings on the compression balances represented the reaction upon the floor. This, however, was not so. Close to the floor, and on the floor, in normal levitation, there in no reaction.

Likewise there is no reaction or pressure on the floor between the table and the medium; for I have often moved my arms, hands, and experimental apparatus freely in this space, and so long as I kept them on or near the floor the phenomenon was not in the least affected.

(4) Besides the reaction on the medium practically equal to the weight of the table, there is a slight reaction upon other members of the circle.

It would appear that about 95 per cent. Of the weight of the table is on the medium and the remaining 5 per cent. on the sitters (Experiments 5 and 6). This involves slight modification of the cantilever theory. The free end is actually not quite free, but is supported very *slightly* by weak cantilevers from other members of the circle. However, the amount of support is so small that it may be neglected.

(5) I have sometimes noticed, during powerful levitation, that if muscular force is applied to the table somewhere in a line towards the medium a solid resistance is encountered,

whereas if the table is depressed vertically an elastic resistance is felt (Experiments 18, 19, 20).

This agrees with the cantilever theory. The beam would be more or less rigid to forces along its length and elastic to forces applied perpendicular to its length.

(6) The cantilever itself, though invisible, may have weight (Experiment 63).

The material of the psychic cantilever, if taken from the medium, would not affect the weight of the medium, as it projects from her and is not supported anywhere over its length. This would agree with all experiments, indicating as they do that during levitation no diminution of the weight of the medium is ever noted.

(7) There is a critical distance of the medium from table required for levitation (Experiment 10). This may have to do with the structure of the cantilever. It is possibly not a simple rod as shown in fig. 24, but may be compounded of several arms, and the coalescing of these arms may require that the medium be not too far from nor too near the table.

(8) I will now go into the puzzling results described in Chapter VII. (Experiments 50 and 53); they are as follows:—

(a) While the séance-table, weight 10 lb., was steadily levitated, there was, upon a compression balance placed centrally on the floor beneath it, a vertical downward force of 30 lb., or 2.89 times the weight of the table; there was also a horizontal pushing force of 5¼ lb. from the medium; and the vertical and horizontal forces were not separate and distinct, but were components of a single force.

(b) While a stool of weight 2 lb. 12 oz., was steadily levitated over a drawing-board placed on top of a compression balance, there was a vertical downward force upon the balance of 18¾ lb., or 6.8 times the weight of the stool.

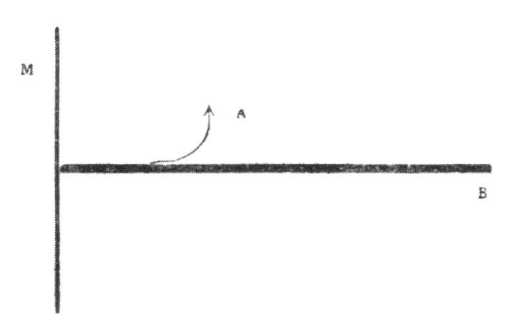

Figure 25

How are these experimental values, of whose practical correctness there can be no doubt, to be explained on the cantilever theory?

Fig. 25 indicates the cantilever A projecting from the medium M. It is shown in its unstrained normal position. The free end B is probably on its under side, within 6 in. of the floor.

Fig. 26 shows the cantilever when in a strained unnatural position owing to the end B having to be raised to the level of the pan of the compression balance. As the beam is elastic, it will in this latter position press *downwards and outwards* on the top of the balance, as indicated by the direction line of the force P. It is obvious that the force P can be resolved into vertical and horizontal components, and I think there can be little doubt that the 30 lb. and 5¼ lb of Experiment 50 are these components.

On this theory, then the stiffness of the structure of the cantilever accounts for the mystifying readings on the compression balances. The reader can form a very fair idea of what is occurring by a simple experiment. Let him take a long flat wooden or steel rule, firmly hold one end, and press the other end against some small article placed above the level of the end which he is holding. When the rule bends, as shown on fig. 26, he will be able to appreciate that he is applying a downward and outward force as mentioned above.

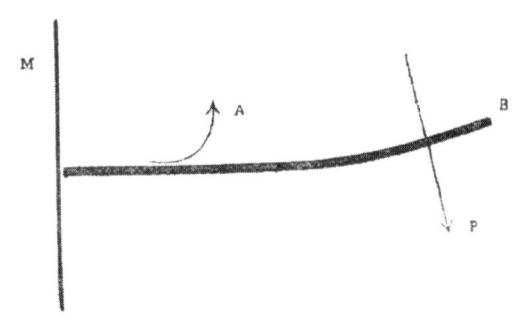

Figure 26

In both experiments both (a) and (b) the height of the platform from which levitation was effected was about the same, viz. 13½ in. and 14 in. respectively. In case (a) the downward force was 30 lb., and in (b) 18¾ lb; why, if the heights are about the same, are the downward forces not the same? The cantilever end would have to be bent upwards practically the same amount in each case. The answer to this, of course, is that the cantilever is not so stiff in case (b) as in (a). The weight of the levitated body in (a) is 10 lb., and in (b) is 2¾ lb. Hence the operators would not require to devise such a stiff cantilever in (b) as in (a), and therefore such a cantilever would be more easily bent upwards from its normal position, and would not exert such a large downward force on the balance.

The following paragraph was written before Experiments 51 and 52 were devised and carried out:—
"The question arises as to how the vertical downward force on the compression balance varies quantitatively with the height of the pan of the balance. If the cantilever proposition be true, I would expect that (1) on the floor there would be no force—which seems from experiment to be the case; (2) as the pan of the balance is gradually raised

in height there would be a position for it when the bottom of the end of the cantilever would be reached, at which point downward force would begin to be registered on the balance; and (3) as the pan is further raised the vertical force would become greater and greater as the end of the cantilever was continually bent upwards."

It is satisfactory to find that when Experiments 51 and 52 were carried out, the three suppositions above mentioned were found to be acutely and literally true. The only thing I found at variance with expectations was that the vertical downward force did not increase in any regular fashion, but there was gradual and then quick and then again a gradual period of increase with varying height. Furthermore, the three tests did not give identical readings for the same size of platform and the same height, yet they gave the same kind of general conclusion. It is not to be expected that the results would be identical, for it is reasonable to suppose that the length of the cantilever would vary somewhat on different evenings, and even at different times on the same evening, and its general shape might be subject to some slight alteration also.

It is seen from fig. 26 that the horizontal component of the outward reaction force on the end of the cantilever is only present when its end is bent upwards. There would be no horizontal component with normal levitation over the floor when the free end is unconstrained. I have not had an opportunity of carrying out experiments for the purpose of discovering the quantitative relation between the horizontal component and the height of the platform, but I expect it would be a gradually increasing one, commencing at zero where the height of the platform was such as to register no vertical reaction, and increasing more or less proportionally with the vertical reaction. I intend, if I have the chance, to carry out this experiment sometime in the future.

Experiments 59 and 60 show clearly that in the space between the medium and the levitated table there are one or more lines or tubes of stress (I think it is better to call them tubes), for the table instantly dropped when the electric contact-maker got in the way, and simultaneously the bell rang, indicating mechanical pressure (although it may be of very small magnitude) from the medium. The tube of stress did not seem to be of very large cross-section, perhaps not more than a few square inches; for I had to move the apparatus here and there in front of the medium before I struck it, and I did not strike it at once. Close to the medium the stress tube was about two feet above the floor (In the neighbourhood of her knees). On the other hand, Experiments 51 and 52 show that under the table mechanical pressure is first apparent on the pan of a compression balance when the pan is about 3 inches above floor level. These two sets of results, therefore, point to a cantilever theory of levitation. They indicate that a cantilever begins somewhere in the body of the medium and projects in a downward direction until it is below the table and a few inches above the floor. All experiments show that on the floor itself, under the table, and between table and medium there is absolutely no pressure, and that the structure is a true cantilever and is not supported anywhere over its length.

The question then arises as to whether the cantilever is straight or curved. Does it resemble a simple straight rod inclining downwards from the medium, or is its shape more complex? On this point I have not such definite evidence as I have on the points already discussed. Reviewing all the experiments and deducing the most likely results, I think the shape of the levitating structure beneath the table is not far off that shown in the accompanying fig. 27, which indicates the cantilever diagrammatically. It consists of two main portions, A and B. A is a slightly curved arm springing from and firmly fixed to the medium M, while B is a vertical column rising from and continuous with its extremity C. The levitated table is supported at the summit T of the column. The reason for the slightly arched shape of the arm is to give additional rigidity to the structure. When the pan of a compression balance is under the table at a height greater than three inches from the floor, the end C presses downwards on it and causes forces to be registered such as those given in the tabulation to Experiments 51 and 52. In Experiments 59 and 60 the electric contact-maker when the bell rang was cutting across the arm A.

I say nothing here as to how a structure possessing the characteristics of a cantilever such as that sketched, and which can support at its extremity for five minutes or more a body weighing 10 lb., can be produced from apparently nothing. I will have something to say about that later on.

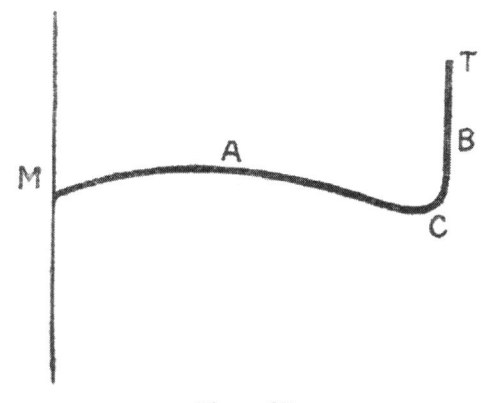

Figure 27

The cantilever above sketched is in my opinion only a particular case of the method by which the operators produce nearly all their phenomena. Levitation of the table is a delicate piece of work, inasmuch as a very nice balance has to be obtained; it is not simply a question of shoving the table here and there without consideration of such things as equilibrium and balance.

Accordingly we find, as might have been expected, that the preliminary operations before levitation occurs at all occupy some little time. A line or physical means of communication seems to be put down from medium to table (see Experiment 64); and when this is "well and truly laid," psychic force is exerted along it (i.e. it is stiffened into a rigid cantilever).

The whole arm A C T in fig. 27 takes the shape shown in order that the particular phenomenon in hand (levitation) may be most accurately accomplished, but that is not the only shape it may have. It is only the best shape for levitation purposes.

Let us suppose that the operators desired to grip the table in the strongest possible manner—that is to say, to move it about the room in the most powerful way in order to impress a visitor who has hold of it by the top and who is endeavouring to prevent motion. What do we find? Turn to Experiment 26.

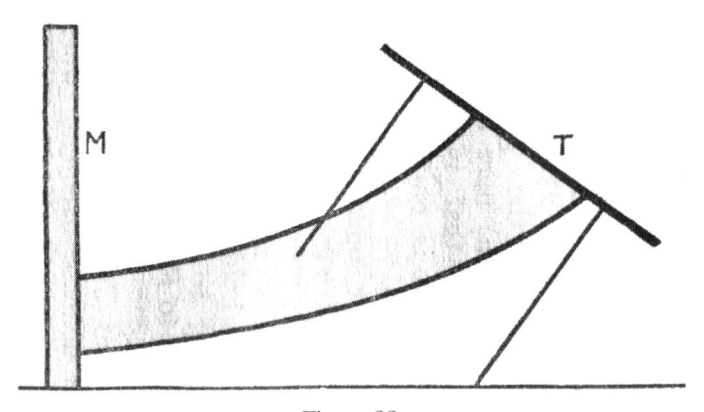

Figure 28

The diagram in that experiment is reproduced in fig. 28. We find that the operators under such conditions, when delicate balancing work is not required, but when magnitude of psychic force is the all-important thing, tilt the edge of the table some 40 degrees with the horizontal in the direction of the medium. I think there can be absolutely no doubt they do this in order that they may take the strongest possible grip with the cantilever arm. No preliminary operations are needed; the table simply tilts, and a short, almost straight arm projects from medium on to the under surface of table.

Many other experiments and observations also suggest that the shape of the cantilever arm required for levitation is only one particular shape of the arm, and that certain other shapes are possible. A very rough analogy is the trunk of an elephant. For delicate levitation work the trunk is made into the shape shown in fig. 27, while for rough powerful work it is made straight, short, and thick. The extremity of the arm projecting from the medium seems able to grip by some adhesive power the wood of the table or certain other articles with which it comes into contact; i.e. there is reason to believe that a levitated table is not simply resting upon the summit of the cantilever column, but that it is firmly fixed to it, as though glued. The following experiments on psychic pull and push will make this matter and other matters dealt with in this chapter clearer; for it often happens that observations of the most elementary nature give us information of the highest importance where so little has been done and so much remains to be accomplished.

Experiment 68: To make some investigations on the psychic pull.

When the séance table stands on the floor within the circle the operators can pull it along the floor right up to the body of the medium.

How is this done?

Fig. 29 gives the position of the table with reference to the medium. M N represents its long edge. Round the legs of the top runs the framework, about 2½ in. deep (not shown). The table was placed within the circle on the floor so that its length M N was parallel to the front of the mediums body, with its nearest edge about 2 ft. distant from her. I stood behind the table directly opposite her. I said to the operators, "Please pull table in towards medium." I slightly held the edge nearest me. The table was immediately pulled in towards the medium, but it did not go in with the edge M N parallel to her body. As it began to move, the corner N got ahead, and consequently the motion was a more or less corner wise one. I said to the members of the circle, "It looks as though the leg (at N) has something to do with the movement. Let us see if the table can be pulled in from the other corner M." No sooner had I spoken than the operators pulled it in towards the medium with the corner M projecting and the table tending to turn about that corner.

Figure 29

I said to the operators, "Have you a rod projecting round one of the legs, and do you pull the table in that fashion?" Answer, vehemently, "No." Question: "Can you pull the table in to the medium so that the edge M N remains parallel to her body, and so that the table does not go in cornerwise with one leg in advance of the other? "This was no sooner asked than the table was pulled in as I desired, with the edge M N parallel to her body during the whole movement. It was done half a dozen times, so that I might make quite certain of it. The table could be pulled right up to her body until it was in contact with her, or the forward motion could be stopped at any instant or at any desired place. There could, therefore, be no doubt that the table could be drawn in straight to the medium in such a way that it was difficult to imagine anything in the nature of a slightly flexible rod getting round a leg. I (and members of the circle, including the medium) began to ask questions of the operators and comment on how it was done. We asked if a grip was taken behind the framework. They answered "No." We exhausted all the methods we could think of for applying a direct pull round any projection. The uniform reply was, "No." They said the grip was taken on *the under surface of the table.* At last I asked, "Is the table brought in by a suction effect?" There were immediately three loud and almost joyous raps in the affirmative. Further inquires and tests make me almost certain that it is even as the operators say. What happens is, in my estimation, as follows (see fig. 27):— The cantilever arm gets under the table—probably a more or less straight arm in this case, as there is little stress. Whatever the physical composition of the substratum of the end of the arm may be, it has the power to take an adhesive grip on certain surfaces, such as wood, with which it comes into contact. The broader columnar end of the arm grips adhesively the under surface of the table, and the operators simply pull the whole psychic arm into the body of the medium. In other words, the psychic arm or cantilever can be moved straight into and out from the body of the medium—can be absorbed in her or projected from her.

Let me now state the motions which are possible to the table standing on the floor within the circle—motions which I have experimentally verified in every case. The table may be moved by psychic force:—

(1) Directly inwards towards medium until it is in contact with her body; (2) directly outwards from medium: (3) in a sideways direction either to right or left (this is a very common movement, for if, during the levitation experiments, I place the table on the floor not exactly in the position desired by the operators, they promptly move it a

little to one side); (4) practically any direction within the circle, as is evidently possible from combinations of the three principle movements enumerated in (1), (2), and (3).

Returning now to the psychic pull. In Experiment 68 the table was pulled directly inwards towards medium, against friction.

Experiment 69: To investigate the psychic pull when the table is lifted.

I lifted the table into the air and asked the operators to pull in as before, which they did immediately. The pull was very perceptible, and, contrary to my expectations, its place of application seemed somewhat low down under the table, perhaps about a foot above the floor. Several tests gave the same kind of result. Moreover, the pulling body (if I may so express it) seemed to my sense of feeling as though it were pretty solid and not at all soft and elastic. The table, in fact, was well and solidly gripped. Now, the cantilever theory shows a psychic arm like this—

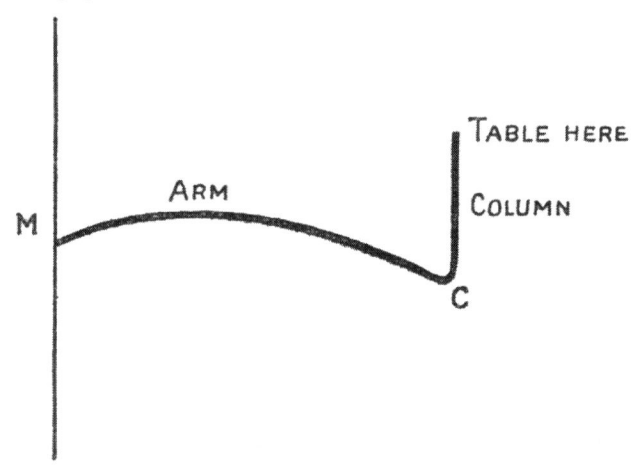

Figure 30

Can the psychic pull be explained on this theory? I think so. The column gets under the table and grips by adhesion its under surface; the operators then absorb the arm bit by bit into the body of the medium, the whole cantilever being thus continually shortened, and finally disappearing into the body of the medium; the place of application of the pulling force is C, at the foot of the column, and this accounts for the direction of pull appearing to be from well beneath the surface of the table. The psychic push is the opposite process, the cantilever being pushed out from the body of the medium. The arm can also move to and fro sideways. It is thus obvious that the arm has a range of action practically over the whole region within the circle, as well as over a considerable space outside the circle in the vicinity of the medium.

Let us now apply the cantilever theory to some more of the experimental results with regard to levitation and see how it fits in.

Take the case of the four tables levitated over the platform of the weighing-machine (Chapter VI). Two of these tables were levitated with the surface practically level, and two with the surface at angles of about 30 degrees with the horizontal. It is to be noted it was with the smaller-sized tables (tables 3 and 4) that the inclination occurred. Does it not seem likely that the operators experienced difficulty in getting their levitating structure properly beneath these tables, owing to the relatively small area of surface and to the fact that the tables were resting on the top of the platform of the machine, a height of about 7 in.? And in that consequence the cantilever, instead of being what I may call the standard shape of fig. 27, was for convenience more like fig. 31?

The reader should bear in mind that the thickness of the arm shown in figs. 27-31 has no significance. The real thickness of the arms is probably very much greater than that sketched. Perhaps being in the vicinity of that shown in fig. 32.

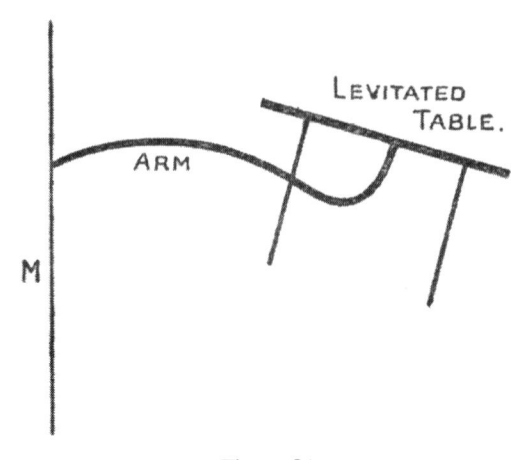

Figure 31

The part A is probably narrow, and the arm broadens and deepens out below the table at B; the part A may even consist of two or three arms springing from various parts of the body of the medium and coalescing into one large portion in the neighbourhood of the table.

The cantilever theory throws some light on the anomalous results of Chapter VI. In the case of the levitation of the stool over the platform of the weighing-machine, it will be remembered that the steelyard was quite stiff during the levitation, and immediately regained its sensitiveness when the levitation was over (Experiment 43). Probably what was happening was that the levitating structure was inclined at some such angle as is shown in fig 31, with the consequence that there was a rather heavy horizontal component of the reaction which pushed the platform over its bearings and caused friction; for it must be remembered that to suit special cases and conditions the levitating cantilever is likely to assume various shapes and forms in conformity to the principle of least work, and that thereby the magnitude and direction of reaction under it are liable to vary.

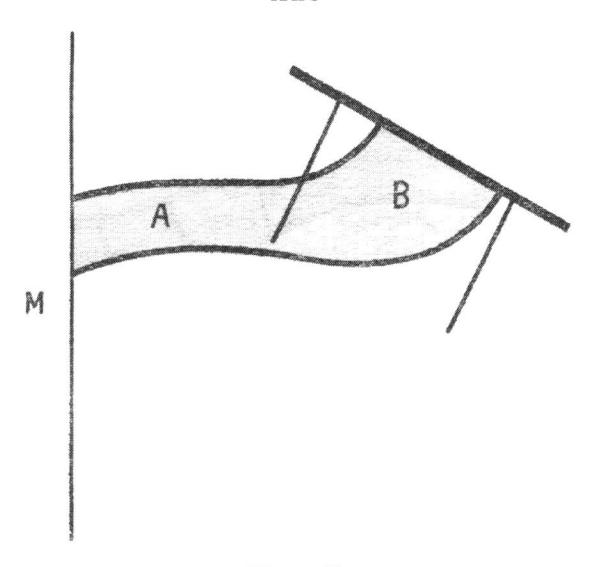

Figure 32

In Experiment 55 it was shown that while a compression balance on the floor under the table was registering vertical reaction during levitation, the medium herself was heavier than she normally is. Unfortunately, I did not find the actual increase of her weight for this levitation, which increase was probably due to the strained condition of the cantilever.

In Experiment 57 a thud was heard on the under surface of the table just before levitation. Is this not likely to have been the top of the broad column beneath the table being applied rather more vigorously than usual to the under-surface? When I remarked on the thud it was immediately repeated for my edification. I take it that it was audible demonstration of the preliminary preparation required for the phenomenon.

In Experiment 24 I have shown that the table may be turned upside down on the floor, and that the experimenter may seize hold of the legs and try to lift it and be unable to do so. Fig. 33 shows what probably happens in that case.

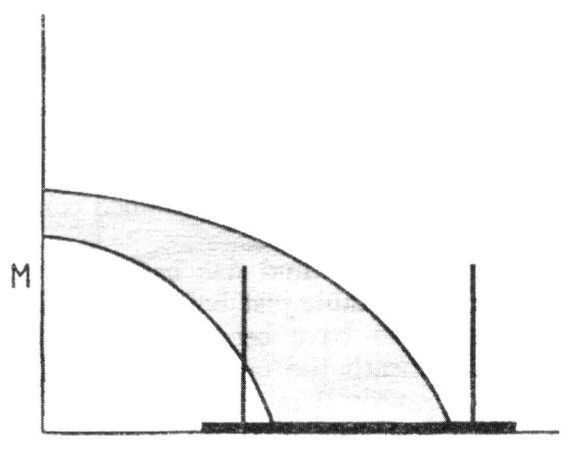

Figure 33

The psychic arm emanating from medium broadens out on to the under surface of table and presses directly upon it, for it must be remembered that experiment shows the arm may (1) push directly outwards from medium, (2) pull directly inwards, (3) move about with medium as fulcrum within the circle. For levitation and similar phenomena the arm is locked (fixed) within the body of the medium.

In Experiment 29 I held a small metal trumpet out into the air, and in a short time it was given a strong forward pull that almost snatched it from my grip. What happened then was, on the present theory, That a psychic arm was projected from the medium, and the end of this, after a little manœuvring, gripped by adhesion the end of the trumpet; the arm was then pulled quickly into the body of the medium; and so strong was the pull that the adhesion gave way and the experimenter only felt a sudden snatch. It is to be noted that some twenty seconds elapsed from the commencement of this experiment until the jerk occurred, indicating that a period of preparation was needed, much in the way that a period of preparation is required for levitation.

I have sometimes observed another experiment with the trumpet which has interesting features in connection with it.

Experiment 70: The trumpet waving to and fro in the air and endeavouring to place itself on the surface of the table.

The trumpet is, at the commencement of the séance, placed on the floor under the table. After a while it rises and the thin end projects well from below the table (fig. 34) on the side remote from the medium and waves to and fro in the air horizontally, beating time to a tune for five minutes or more. This has happened many times. But the next process is not so common—I have only seen it some three times. After waving about in the air for some time, the small end of the trumpet—that projecting beyond the table— rises until it touches the edge of the table, then the trumpet slides bodily up the ledge, by short sharp jerks, at the same time bending over to the top surface, while the thick end comes out from below the table.

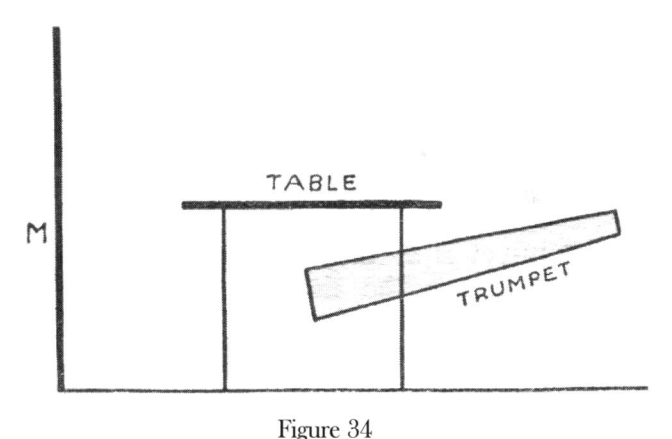

Figure 34

Three successive positions are shown on fig. 35 which will make the description clearer. When it gets into the position (3), the whole trumpet can be clearly seen apparently in contact with nothing. Further strong shoves are then given it in an endeavour to slide it up the ledge and jerk it on to the surface of the table. I myself have observed the trumpet one step farther advanced on its journey than (3), but I have not seen the actual completion of the experiment. On the occasions I have witnessed the phenomenon the operators were unable to succeed with the final necessary jerk. However the sitters inform me that it has been completely successful on one occasion.

I take it that the psychic arm had hold of the trumpet by adhesion to its thick end, and that the various motions given to it were more or less those I have dealt with already.

This experiment of the movement of the trumpet, the waving to and fro in the air keeping time to a tune, and the motions described above about the ledge of the table may be interesting to those who at "dark" séances have heard the "voices" through the trumpet which was presumably moving about the room.

In Experiment 22 it was stated that when the table stands on the floor within the circle it can be made on request almost as light as a feather or so heavy that it cannot be lifted.

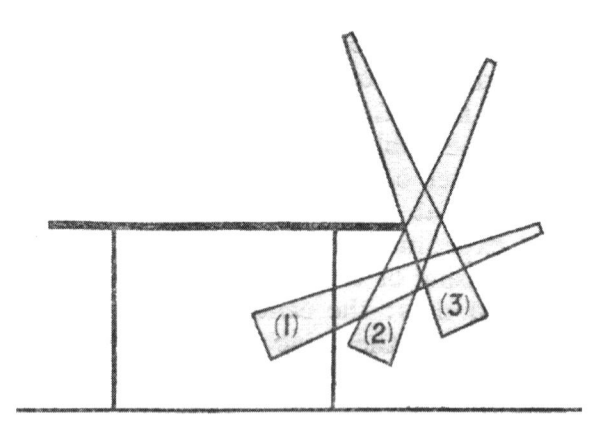

Figure 35

Now, it has been shown (Chapter VII, Experiments 45, 47, etc.) that when a compression balance is on the floor below the table, if, say, 30 lb. is the normal vertical reaction for steady levitation, this reaction is not applied suddenly, but, in other words grows steadily for about five to six seconds, and that the table seems to spring into the air when the growth of psychic force is complete. According to the cantilever theory this growth of the reaction is synonymous with the making of the cantilever rigid enough to withstand the weight of the levitated table. Suppose, now, that the growth of this psychic force is stopped at a value which does not make the cantilever sufficiently rigid to lift the table, but which nevertheless makes it sufficiently strong to exert a considerable upward force on the table—but less than its weight,—then we have the apparent decrease of the weight of the table explained. The operators can as a matter of fact stop the growth of the psychic force at any magnitude they wish, as abundant experimental results amply testify.

The increasing of the weight of the table may be explained thus: the cantilever end grips the under surface of the table by adhesion, and is then pressed downwards towards the floor.

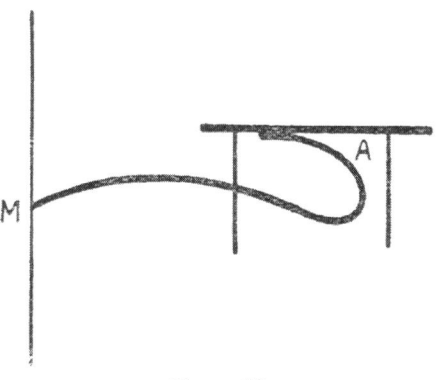

Figure 36

A point I have already remarked on several times is the fact that when the psychic pressure becomes sufficiently great, the table seems actually to *spring* into the air. It does not rise gradually, as might have been supposed. The experimenter almost feels, when he watches it, that some restraining force had been suddenly removed which was keeping it from levitating. Perhaps the following idea, which seems to me at least feasible, may partly explain it:—

During the preparation for levitation the line of communication (whatever it may consist of) is loose and soft; a flexible connection A is made with the under surface of the table (fig. 36).

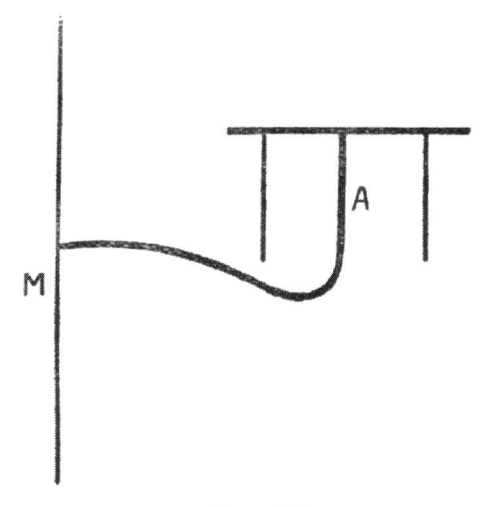

Figure 37

Psychic force is extended along the line and a stiff cantilever is gradually formed. At a certain instant, depending upon the rigidity attained by the end A, the end A suddenly opens out (fig. 37) and becomes straight and vertical. As it is attached to the table, the latter of course rises with it and appears to levitate with a jerk or spring.

CHAPTER X

RAPS

At my experimental circles all kinds and degrees of rapping occurred, varying in sound from the slightest audible ticks to blows such as might have been produced (judging by the noise) by a sledge-hammer; dances and tunes were rapped out on the floor or table, sounds as of a bouncing ball were heard in the room, the leg of the table was apparently sawn, the floor was rubbed as though with sand-paper, a man was heard walking and a horse trotting over the floor, and so on (see Chapter I).

I intend now to describe the experimental work I have carried out in connection with this matter, and to evolve a theory to account for it.

Experiment 71: The medium sitting quietly on the weighing-machine, to observe how her weight was affected when rapping was occurring.

The small, accurate weighing-machine described in Chapter III, lent by Messrs W. & T. Avery, Ltd., was used. The drawing-board (see Chapter III) was tied to the platform and a piece of dark carpet was tacked to it, as there was reason to believe that white light rays from its surface were interfering with the intensity of the phenomena. The circle sat throughout the experiments with hands on knees, so that each member was physically isolated from the rest. The mediums hands were flat on her knees, and at my request she sat perfectly still.

Initial weight of medium + chair + drawing-board .... = 9 st. 4 lb. 0 oz.

Having balanced accurately, I asked the operators to rap on the floor, as I wished to discover if a rap synchronised with increase or decrease of weight as registered on the weighing-machine. One or two raps were given, but of an intensity only just audible. Thereafter there were raps at intervals of a few seconds. As they became gradually louder I noticed a peculiar effect. Sometimes coinciding with each rap or blow on the floor the steelyard would rise against the top stop, and would sometimes fall against the bottom stop. I did not understand what was going on until I noticed that the weight of the medium as balanced between the raps was diminishing. With the increasing loudness of raps the weight of the medium continued to decrease, this process going on until the loudest sledge-hammer blows were being given, when the weight became stationary and did not decrease further, and thereafter, until the end of the experiment, remained steady. The time occupied in the process was about a minute.

Final weight of medium + chair + drawing-board .... = 8 st.10 lb. 0 oz.
Therefore final steady decrease in weight .... = 8 lb.

When conditions became steady I informed the operators that I was going to watch the process again. I accordingly turned on white light rays into the circle, which process always effectively prevents phenomena. Then I weighed medium, chair and drawing-board again. The new weight was 9 st. 4 lb. I then asked the operators to "set conditions" and to rap at intervals. Again the weight began gradually to decrease and the loudness of the raps to increase, the loudness, so far as could be judged, being directly proportional to decrease of weight. When sledge-hammer intensity was reached, the weight became steady again at 8 st. 10 lb. It seems therefore necessary to conclude that (1) raps, blows, etc., cannot be produced unless the mediums weight is reduced; (2) the intensity of the rap depends upon the decrease of weight and is apparently directly proportional to it; (3) the loss of weight is merely temporary, as on each occasion of re-weighing after the experiment the initial dead weight of 9 st. 4 lb. was obtained; (4) the loss of weight is not effected suddenly, but on the contrary quite gradually; (5) after a time the loss of weight reaches a final amount and thereafter does not vary.

It seems to me that the loss represents actual matter temporarily detached from the medium and used in some manner in the production of raps, blows, etc.

Experiment 72: The effects of raps, blows, etc., given on the floor, upon the weight of the medium.

Initial weight of medium + chair + drawing-board .... = 9 st. 4 lb. 0 oz.

When the reduction in weight, as mentioned in Experiment 71, had reached a maximum, and the steelyard balanced at 8 st. 10 lb., I asked the operators to produce raps of various intensities on the floor. The results were as follows: Raps of all degrees of loudness cause corresponding and synchronous increase of weight of medium, indicated by steelyard pressing for a second against the top stop, the pressure roughly proportional to loudness of rap, varying from the slightest upward movement of steelyard to a force (as judged by the sense of touch) of many pounds. Impacts on the floor, such as the bouncing ball imitation, sand-paper noise on floor, and so on (Chapter I) all cause synchronous and temporary additional weight, the lever again balancing after each blow.

How are we to reconcile the results of Experiment 71 and the experiments dealing with levitation, where in the one case the medium loses weight and in the other gains it? The only reasonable conclusion is that the process during levitation is different from that during the production of raps and impacts generally. During the process of levitation I have never observed any initial or other decrease in the weight of the medium, but, on the contrary, always an increase. Again, in Experiment 71 the operators knew that raps and blows only were expected, and no levitation was attempted; hence it is to be presumed that the reduction in weight then noted was that necessary for the work in hand alone. Also I would add that during levitation raps are very seldom given, and then only of the feeblest type.

Experiment 73: What happened to the medium's weight at the commencement of a séance, and the effect of rapping, etc.

In this experiment (which was carried out at a later date than Experiments 71 and 72) I am going to describe what occurred near the commencement of a séance in which for some reason or other—perhaps partly owing to the extremely wet weather—phenomena were slower than usual in getting under way. Probably the processes noted in this case occur during all séances, but on ordinary occasions they are soon finished and psychical equilibrium is quickly established. On the present occasion, after the circle had held hands in the chain formation for some little time and a few levitations had been obtained, I seated the medium on the chair on the weighing-machine. I then altered the chain order and asked each member of the circle to place hands on knees. Owing to the somewhat unfavourable conditions prevailing, this seemed to break up what psychic balance had existed, with the consequence that, to all intents and purposes, the séance had to commence over again. The initial weight of medium + chair + drawing-board was 9 st. 10 lb. 12 oz. I carefully watched the balance of the weighing-machine. During the first five minutes or so there was no decrease or increase of weight registered, and no replies by raps in answer to repeated requests. Then the weight began very slowly to diminish, and light raps began to be heard. I wish to emphasise the fact that until this first slight diminution in weight occurred, absolutely no raps were given. Soon after the process had commenced the weight began to decrease in successive fluxes of from 2 lb. to 5 lb. or slightly more, and at the termination of each decrease to come back somewhat. It would seem that as soon as a little weight is removed the drawing action upon the medium becomes easier; in other words, that the establishing of even a weak psychic field facilitates greatly the preliminary operations. The process once started, I asked the operators to rap at intervals. The fluxes of decreasing weight continued, becoming gradually greater and greater. I noticed that when a loud blow was given on the floor the weight would greatly diminish—as much as 20 lb. or even more—and would usually come back, to what it was before the blow was struck. The weight did not flow back instantly after the blow, but if it did come back it did so slowly, taking perhaps six or seven seconds. Now and then it did not come back for about half a minute, and on those occasions it did not return so far as the original amount registered before the blow. The weight, generally speaking, decreased in waves, irregularly (see fig. 38).

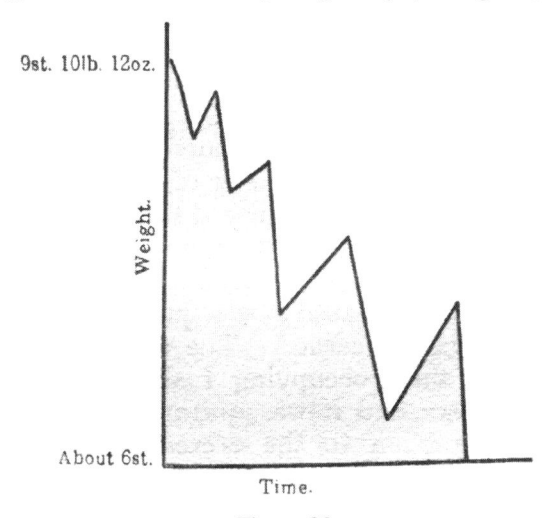

Figure 38

The final fairly steady value—which lasted for a few minutes—was about 6 st., although there were fluxes somewhat below this.

It seems to me that in this experiment we witness two processes in combination:—

(1) The process of getting the medium into condition—the loosening of the psychic stuff by strong fluxes of upward force upon her body; and (2) the removal of sufficient material from her body for the production of raps.

When the processes outlined above had been going on for about a quarter of an hour, and the total weight had been fairly steady at about 6 st. for a minute or so, the medium began to regain her lost weight. I watched the process with great interest, because it was quite unexpected so far as I was concerned. The regaining process was very slow, occupying I should say about two minutes, and it was quite regular, in sharp contradistinction to the decreasing process. I quite easily kept the lever balanced by the rider as the weight grew, and I followed it up until exactly the original value of 9 st. 10 lb. 12 oz. was reached.

I expect that in ordinary séances, with conditions normal, the initial drawing process is finished very quickly. The final action, that in which the medium gradually regained her weight, was probably the conclusion of the preliminary operations, for phenomena soon started, and proceeded with much their usual vigour. The results of this experiment seem to me to give us some positive notions as to the meaning of the fluxes of nervous and muscular stress so many people experience at the opening of a séance.

There is just the possibility that the operators were acting directly upon the lever of the weighing-machine. The chances against this are however, very great. The operators knew that to do so would be to render the results valueless; they were as keen on the experiments as myself, and if at any time they were unable to carry out any test they always told me. Moreover, during much of the time I had fairly strong light upon the lever of the machine. Then the correspondence between the loudness of the raps and the decrease of weight, the synchronism between the raps and the fluxes of decreased weight, and so on, all show quite plainly that the forces registered were due to actions upon the medium alone.

It is fairly evident that the main processes included in levitation of the table and in rapping are somewhat different; indeed, an actual temporary loss of the medium's weight seems essential for rapping (Experiments 71 and 73), and furthermore the intensity of the rap seems directly proportional to the amount of the loss of weight. I have on several occasions noted the distinction between the two processes, and at one séance in my own house I made some particular observations on it.

Experiment 74: Distinction between the levitation and rapping processes.

Levitation phenomena had been in progress for some time. Just after a levitation was over I asked a question of the operators. There was no answer for half a minute or so. Then a reply was given by gentle raps. In a few seconds the raps increased in intensity, and before long were sharp and distinct—that is to say, the change from the processes involved in levitation to those made use of in rapping required time. I watched this change on several occasions on this particular evening, and I had observed it often before. I am now quite certain that it takes appreciable and measurable time to effect. As further corroboration, I have noted that sometimes, instead of going to the trouble of "changing over," the operators would prefer to answer questions by tilting the end of the table, which is a much more cumbersome method of holding a conversation than the method of raps.

Experiment 75: "Bombardment" of the medium during rapping.

This experiment was conducted in my own house. The medium was sitting at the head of the circle, and I placed myself almost directly opposite her. The light was good, and I could observe her thoroughly. The operators were producing heavy thuds on the floor in front of her at intervals of a few seconds. At each thud the medium was pushed backwards on her chair—even violently pushed backwards, for the movement was quite obvious. She seemed to be struck in the region of the chest, and the motion given to her was very similar to that given to any large body which, being free to move, is struck by a small one travelling with considerable velocity. In other words, a back force seemed to react on her for each rap. I watched the process for quite a long time, and the result was never in doubt. When the raps became lighter and quicker, she still received pushes which caused her to swing backwards—motions which were quite visible, evidently one for each rap; and at one time she was under a veritable bombardment from the reactions. When the raps were produced in her immediate neighbourhood, instead of out in the circle, I noticed that she seemed to be hit in more nearly a vertical direction than was the case for the latter position—that is, the reaction for the rap seems to be transmitted from the floor in a straight line to somewhere near the chest of the medium. If the rap is produced far out in the circle, this straight line is not so much inclined to the floor as when it is produced near the medium; all of which is very natural and in agreement with the laws of mechanics if we suppose something in the nature of a semi-rigid body or rod projects itself from the medium to the point on the floor where the rapping is to occur.

In addition to observing the bombardment of the medium, I went over to her while it was in progress and felt the various motions of her body. She experiences no inconvenience from the rap reactions, and nothing of the stress she undergoes when a table levitates.

Experiment 76: To endeavour to discover the "Shape" of a rap.

In order to test the result of a rap on paper, I procured a couple of brass rings about six inches in diameter, placed a piece of brown paper between them, and fixed the rings together by a couple of bolts through projecting lugs. The paper was then taut, somewhat like the end of drum. The rap was duly delivered upon the paper, which on examination was found to be indented heavily, and slightly torn downwards in a curved line about an inch long, as though it had received a slanting blow from something of an oval shape about two square inches in area and moving comparatively slowly.

CHAPTER XI

THE ROD THEORY FOR RAPS

The theory to account for the phenomenon of raps which I am now going to discuss is as follows:—

From various parts of the body of the medium psychic semi-flexible rods are projected, the end portions of which, being struck sharply on the floor, table, chair, or other body, cause the sharp sounds known generally as raps.

These rods apparently all the characteristics of solid bodies; they are more or less flexible, and can be varied in length and diameter. Several of the smaller rods, or one of the largest size, may project from the medium at any one time. Each one, especially near its extremity, is more or less rigid, and the rigidity can be varied within limits depending upon conditions of light, the psychic energy available, and so forth. The rigidity is probably ultimately brought about by some kind of molecular action concerning which we are as yet perfectly ignorant—the kind of action that produces the same effect on the cantilever.

I have heard of various "explosion" theories for raps. I disagree completely with all such. If what occurs at my circle is typical—and I expect it is—there is not the vestige of any evidence for explosions, but, on the other hand, an overwhelming testimony for direct impacts by a body resembling a solid one. Let me go over some of this evidence in detail.

(1) The raps (by which term I include little light raps, knocks, sledgehammer blows, and all intermediate varieties) cause vibration of the floor or other body upon which they are produced. The heavier blows cause such pronounced vibration that the boards of the floor sensibly shake. All visitors to the séance room notice this.

(2) *The Psychic Touch:* Touches are sometimes experienced at the circle. I have carefully analysed their

impression on the sense of feeling. A psychic touch feels exactly as though the rounded end of a material rod was pushed on one's arm, or foot, or other part of the body. The "solidity" of the touching body is what impresses the experimenter; for no matter how carefully or softly the operators apply the touch, one feels as though the blunted end of a hard something—a something even made of metal—were being used. On my theory this touching apparatus is, in fact, the end of a "rapping" rod projecting from the medium, the end of a rod which in some unknown manner is made half rigid. When the experimenter has felt this unexpectedly solid touch he begins to understand a little about the process of the rap in general.

(3) The rigidity of the rapping rod varies with the amount of light to which it is subjected. This statement may appear curious. Perhaps I had better illustrate by an example. Sometimes we have formed an impromptu circle in the dining-room or other room where a fire was burning and where light was coming in through the blinds from street lamps outside. On such occasions the operators either rap on the medium's chair or on the floor between her chair and that of Mr. Morrison—that is to say, in either case in close proximity to the medium. When at such times the light is too strong or is badly regulated (as usually happens), the raps resemble soft, dull thuds, and cannot seemingly be made sharp and distinct. I cannot overcome the conviction that the rapping rod in such cases is not so rigid as usual; that in fact it becomes soft, or even, as it were, partially melted on its periphery, where it is exposed to the light, and that its core is the only part of it remaining solid. Hence the dull, softish sound of its free end when it strikes the floor.

(4) The rapping rods issue from various parts of the body of the medium. When the amount of psychic energy is low, or when the quantity available is small, such as near the commencement of a séance, the rods are naturally of the

shortest length possible consistent with the production of the phenomenon. Accordingly, at the beginning of operations in the séance room the raps are first heard quite close to the medium's feet, for the rods in that case issue, as I have reason to believe, from her ankles or from some part in close proximity. My reason for thus locating the starting-place of such rods is due to the mechanical reactions of the raps (Experiments 72, 73). These particular mechanical reactions cause her to make slight involuntary motions with her feet, motions which a careless observer would set down to imposture. After a little time, when further stores of psychic energy become available, the raps are produced further out in the circle—on the chairs of the sitters, or on the under surface of the table within the circle. The starting-point of the rod then seems to be much higher up her body, for the reactionary movements are then visible on the trunk.

(5) Raps vary in intensity from the slightest audible sounds to blows such as could be struck—judging by the sound—by a sledge-hammer. (Of course, the intensity of the latter blows is not that which would be obtained from an actual sledge-hammer, or the floor-boards would be split. I expect the end of the rod in such cases "gives," i.e. is slightly elastic, with the result that only violent vibration of the floor occurs, and that there is in reality more noise than actual force.)

The beating of a carpet by a flexible cane seems to be somewhat analogous to the actual process.

I have noted often that the heaviest blows are not usually delivered quickly. Two such blows are seldom struck in series—that is, one following the other immediately, in the manner of what is called the double knock. There is an interval of a second or two between them, and while the blows are in progress no other phenomena can be produced. On my theory, what is here happening is that one large rod is projecting from the medium, a rod of such large dimensions that the psychic energy available is used in its construction. In other words, it is a sledge-hammer and not a tack-hammer. When the raps required are light, two or more thin rods may be projecting from the medium simultaneously. Take the case of a jig or other complicated tune being rapped out on floor or table. The raps follow each other so quickly that it is reasonable to suppose that the operator has at his command a series of projecting rods, and uses these as we would use the keys of a piano. Some of the rods used must be very thin. At a rough guess I should say they vary from a diameter of about ⅛ in. to one of 2 in, or 3 in.

(6) I have carefully watched the phenomenon of raps while the medium has been seated on the weighing-machine. If the reader will refer to Experiments 71, 72, and 73, he will find some relative data. The conclusions from those experiments were as follows:—

(a) Raps, blows, etc., cannot be produced unless the medium's weight is reduced.

(b) The intensity of the rap depends upon the medium's decrease of weight, and is apparently directly proportional to it.

In experiment 73 I state: "I wish to emphasise the fact that until this first slight diminution in weight occurred, absolutely no raps were given." Also, "I noticed that when a loud blow was given on the floor the weight would greatly diminish—as much as 20 lb. or more—and would then usually come back, to what it was before the blow was struck." Hence it will be seen that in this experiment a state of equilibrium had evidently not been arrived at, as was seemingly the case in Experiment 71, where a maximum steady diminution of weight of about 8 lb. was maintained during the loudest blows, and where there did not appear to be fluxes of weight diminution accompanying the blows.

Let us see how the matter works out on the rod theory.

The diminution of weight: The rigidity of the psychic rod is due in some way to material particles temporarily projected from the medium. So soon as a rod is formed, its free end rests on the floor, i.e. part of the body of the medium is supported on the floor beyond the weighing-machine on which she is seated; she thus apparently loses weight. The thicker the rod the more of the matter of her body is thus externally supported, and, as the thickness of the rod used determines the intensity of the rap, her apparent loss of weight is thus proportional to the intensity of the blow.

In Experiment 71 with perfect psychic equilibrium, it was found that, during the period of experimenting for the loudest blows, the medium's weight remained practically at a diminution of 8 lb. With the steelyard of the weighing-machine balanced at this diminution, it was found that raps caused corresponding and synchronous increase of weight of the medium, indicated by steelyard pressing for a second against the top stop, the pressure being roughly proportional to loudness of rap, varying from slightest upward movement of steelyard to a force—as judged by the sense of touch—of many pounds. In my opinion this temporary increase of weight was caused (1) by one or more of the rods being lifted from the floor, and (2) by the mechanical reaction on the medium when the rod was impacted on the floor to cause the rap.

This reaction is a very real matter, and affords further evidence that something mechanical, most likely in the nature of a more or less flexible rod, is in reality used.

(7) Besides the usual raps, blows, etc., there are various peculiar modifications. For instance, there is the imitation of the bouncing ball, which is so lifelike that the listener would be prepared to declare that a material ball is really present. How is this imitation accounted for on the rod theory? Probably there is some modification of the terminal

of the rod. It is made softer than usual, and its shape is perhaps altered somewhat also.

The imitation of sand-paper rubbing the floor is not hard to understand. The end of a rod is rubbed along the floor instead of impacting on it.

The imitation of the table leg being sawn is more difficult. Perhaps this is caused by the rod being moved lengthwise across the leg of the table, i.e. the end of the rod is not used, but the axial surface of it.

(8) The movements of small objects "without contact" is generally understandable on the rod theory. When the little hand-bell is lifted, as often happens, a couple of rods may be supposed to seize it on either side like a pair of tongs, or a single rod may grip it by adhesion. That such rods have more or less the characteristics of solid bodies may be seen in an experiment with the bell. Sometimes when the bell is lifted it does not ring clearly, but has the dulled sound one would obtain if it were gripped by the metal instead of the handle. The rod, or rods, are in that case pressing against the metal, and, as they have the properties of solid bodies, they damp the sound vibrations. But the bell can evidently be also seized by the handle, when it rings clearly in the ordinary manner. Sometimes the operators ring the bell and rap on the floor simultaneously.

I will now describe a couple of curious experiments in connection with raps, which illustrate some of the points discussed above.

Experiment 77: The typewriter experiment.

I wished to see what the operators could do with a typewriter placed within the circle; whether the keys could be struck with the precision necessary to imprint letters upon the paper; whether the mass of metal of which the machine was composed would have a deleterious effect; whether a rational message could be typed out; and so on. Accordingly, a Barlock typewriter having been kindly placed at my disposal by Mr. T. Edens Osborne, I fixed a sheet of paper in it in the ordinary way, and placed it on the floor near the centre of the circle. No sooner had I done so and turned on the red light, than the keys were struck lightly and rapidly as though a pair of hands were playing over them. This having continued for some little time, I examined the mechanism, but I found that the type levers had become jammed, evidently from several keys having been struck simultaneously, and these had to be disengaged before the experiment could be proceeded with. (The typewriter was rather an old-fashioned one and somewhat complex.) It was apparent that the operators did not know how to use the machine. I therefore explained to them that they must strike each key separately with a sharp blow and allow time for it to come back to its normal position before striking another. They followed this advice carefully on the next occasion—with an exactness that was even surprising—and succeeded in typing the following:—

mbx; gesq'

There is nothing in the nature of a message in the foregoing, and the experiment is chiefly interesting as showing that the keys can be struck with just the force necessary to produce such a result. The mass of metal composing the typewriter seems to have no injurious effects on the transmission and application of the force. I will add that the letters on the keys were in some cases much worn; perhaps the operators found some difficulty in reading them.

Experiment 78: I smoothed out a lump of rather soft putty into a saucer on the floor near the middle of the circle. I asked the operators to "rap" on the putty. Three impressions were made on it. They were similar in form, each consisting of an oblong cavity about ¾ in. long and ½ in. wide at its widest part, sloping down gradually from the periphery to a maximum depth of ¼ in. or so. The near edges of the two outside impressions impinged upon the middle one. The floor of each cavity was not smooth, but was lined by two series of grooves or waves (although I call them "waves," I do so for convenience of description only; the reader should understand that I have no intention of asserting that the pulse is transmitted in wave form): (a) long, comparatively deep waves, and (b) waves crossing the crests of the former at right angles. The long waves were all practically parallel to one another and straight for the greater portion of their length, though they showed a tendency to curl round near the long ends of the cavity.

Figure 39

Fig. 39 represents diagrammatically three of the long waves A, B, C, near the middle of the cavity. The dark lines represent the crests, and the white spaces the troughs of the waves, which are nearly equally spaced. Three cross waves are shown by the lines, 1, 2, 3. Careful measurement shows that there are about thirteen of the long waves per inch of width, and about thirty-two cross waves per inch. The latter cut through the crests of the long waves at right angles, and reach a depth of about one third the height of the long wave as measured from trough to crest. The measurements were difficult owing to the curvature of the holes, but are correct approximately.

These waves were evidently not made by a sliding motion parallel to their length, but seem to have been impressed by a force acting approximately perpendicularly to the putty, for the putty is not heaped up or abraded anywhere, as would result if the former were the case.

On thinking the matter over, I remembered that the markings were very similar to those on the human finger and thumb. Accordingly I examined my own fingers and thumb through a magnifying glass. A magnification of three or four diameters indicated a great degree of correspondence. Assuming that the markings were impressions of part of a finger or thumb, it has to be remembered that crests on the finger correspond to troughs in the cavity and vice versa; but even so, there are indications that the cross notches or waves in the cavity are produced by similar notches faintly showing at the base of the troughs of the long waves on the finger. If, then, as seems most likely to me, these "raps" on the putty are really produced by invisible fingers, the following deductions would seem to be implied:—

(a) The impressing fingers are not of a normal size, but are at least three times as large as normal ones. This is evident from a comparison of the pitch and depth of the grooves.

(b) The impressed grooves are so cleanly and regularly cut that we must suppose the impressing fingers are "new" ones i.e. they are in this respect unlike the marks on the human finger, which are more or less worn, as is evident from examination through the magnifying glass.

(c) The impressions are only a small part of the finger or thumb.

(d) The impressions may be due to something resembling the large toe on the human foot; but if so, the deductions (a), (b), and (c) still hold.

Now, what are we to make of this? Does it invalidate the rod theory? Not so far as I can see. The only point of difference would seem to be that the end of the rapping rod in this case was specially prepared with something resembling a finger-print, just as for the bouncing-ball test and the saw test it would also have to be specially modified. I should have thought that the end of the rod for simple rapping would have been plain and unencumbered with design, following out the principle of least work. Accordingly, I interrogated the operators on the matter. They said decisively and repeatedly that the impressions on the putty were finger-prints, but that in ordinary rapping fingerprints were not used; that, in fact, a simple blunt projection was employed. They produced the finger-prints on this occasion to show what they could do and because the putty, being soft, was able to reproduce them.

While on this subject it may interest my readers to hear that when I had worked out the cantilever theory for levitation, I put it to the operators bit by bit as plain and untechnical language as possible. They say the whole thing is practically accurate. They say they understand what I mean when I describe the arched rod issuing from the medium, going below the table, and a column rising from its end, and so forth. They also say the rod theory for raps is substantially accurate. Of course I do not ask anybody to place any scientific value upon this, but only mention it as a matter of interest. Once I asked how the cantilever arms, rapping rods, etc., are made rigid. They said they did not know. I asked them if there were any entities who *did* know. They answered in the affirmative. Asked if they could bring these entities to the circle to impart the information to me, they said they were doubtful if they could do so. Up to now I have heard no more of the matter.

I now describe some experiments with the electroscope on psychic "touching," which in my opinion is only a variation of rapping.

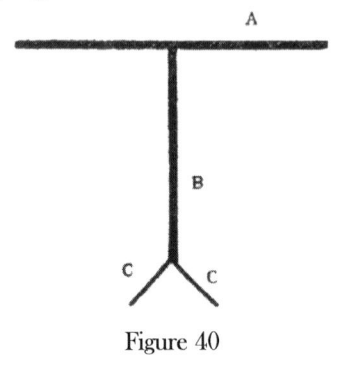

Figure 40

The electroscope used was of a simple type sufficiently illustrated by fig. 40.

A is a thin brass disc, B the brass stem, and CC the gold leaves. The whole is enclosed from a little way below the disc in a protecting box with glass front and back and metal sides. Proper insulation, of course, is provided. For the experiments described below I charged the electroscope on each occasion at a small table in the corner of the room, and then took it to whatever part of the circle I desired. I found that throughout the tests I could never charge the instrument fully, i.e. so that the gold leaves would widely diverge; but that nevertheless I could charge it so that the leaves would open about two thirds their full amount and remain for an indefinite time at that distance apart.

Experiment 79: Electroscope placed under table where psychic energy was supposed to be concentrated.

I charged the electroscope, and then asked the operators to take their attention from the table (they had been levitating it) and to remove as much weight as they could from the body of the medium, and to indicate to me that they had accomplished this by giving a sledge-hammer blow on the floor. The matter removed (used in the production of raps) I asked should be concentrated under the table standing on the floor. In about one minute a terrific blow was given upon the floor as a sign to me that the operation was complete. I then placed the charged electroscope under the table and kept it there for half a minute or so.

Result: The electroscope was unaffected.

Experiment 80: Psychic touching of the disc of the electroscope.

I took the electroscope to the table in the corner, discharged and recharged it. I then placed it within the circle near the centre. I asked the operators to "touch" the disc of the instrument very gently. They did this almost at once, the "touching" consisting of a metallic scraping upon the brass disc, quite audible, similar in type to the imitation of the floor being rubbed with sand-paper, a phenomenon I have often observed.

Result: On examination the electroscope was found to be completely discharged.

Experiment 81: Further test on "touching" of electroscope.

I took the electroscope to the table in the corner of the room and tried to recharge it, but I found I was unable to do so even after repeated trials. Accordingly I asked the operators to put back into the body of the medium the matter they had taken out at my request in Experiment 70 (for the production of sledge-hammer blows), and to give a few raps when they had done so. In a minute or so some *very light raps* were given, and when I asked if the process was complete I *received no raps in reply at all*, which seemed to indicate to me that all the matter used for rapping had been returned to the medium. At any rate, I found that I could now charge the electroscope; which done, I placed it on the floor as before within the circle, and asked that the disc should be "touched" lightly. After a little time there was the metallic scraping as before, and on examination the electroscope was found to be completely discharged.

Experiment 82: Further experiment on "touching" of electroscope.

I repeated experiment 80 most carefully. I found the same difficulty in recharging the electroscope, and the same process had to be gone over again before it could be recharged. When "touched" it was discharged as before.

As a working hypothesis to account for some of the results of Experiments 79-82, it occurs to me that the psychic "touching" of the disc of the electroscope is equivalent to putting the body of the medium in contact with the instrument by means of matter abstracted from her for the production of raps and similar effects. No doubt the scraping action referred to belongs to the rapping category of phenomena; probably the rapping rod is drawn over the surface of the disc instead of impacting it.

CHAPTER XII

MISCELLANEOUS EXPERIMENTS

Experiment 83: Electric shock test.

I placed a small induction coil on the floor within the circle, connected it to a dry cell, and gave the medium one of the terminals to hold in her right hand (the members of the circle were sitting with hands on knees). The other terminal (each of the terminals consisted of a small tube of metal about two inches long) I placed on the floor. Asked the operators to apply psychic force to the terminal on the floor, to "touch" it, and move it about. They appeared to do all these things.

Result: The medium said that on one occasion she felt what she afterwards recognised as a weak electric shock in her right arm, and that her wrist gave a jerk. She was most positive that she felt the shock, though it is evident there is much room for self-suggestion in the experiment. It is true I took care not to let her see the apparatus before the experiment, but, of course, the test is inconclusive, and I only give it as a matter of interest.

Experiment 84: Phosphorescence.

I brought to the séance room a small piece of cardboard which had been covered on one side with powered calcium sulphide, a substance which has the property of phosphorescing for several hours after it has been exposed to sunlight. Previous to the experiment I had kept the cardboard in an envelope in my pocket for twenty-four hours. The gaslight having been turned off in the séance room, we were left in total darkness. I placed the cardboard on the floor within the circle, prepared surface uppermost, and asked the operators to apply psychic force to it, to "touch" it, and to "rap" on it. This they apparently did, judging by the sounds. I then held it in my fingers and asked that it should be pushed. This was done, and I felt the pushes.

Result: Absolutely no sign of phosphorescence.

Experiment 85: Fluorescence.

I also brought an X-ray fluorescent screen (platino-cyanide of barium) to the séance room, and asked the operators to treat it as they had done the prepared cardboard of Experiment 84. They apparently did so.

Result: No sign of fluorescence.

The room being pitch dark at this time—the only occasion in all my experiments,—the operators, at the conclusion of the tests, desired to show us what they could do under such conditions. The result was that a small earthquake seemed to be playing about the room. I need not go into details, but will only say that the table could not be held by any muscular force exerted; it turned upside down and levitated in that fashion (see Experiment 23), and it performed every possible kind of contortion. The blows on the floor were terrific, and such, in fact, was the din that I was glad to light the gas.

Experiment 86: Delicacy of force actions upon the medium.

In Experiment 73 will be found an account of what occurred to the weight of the medium near the commencement of a séance in which phenomena were slow in starting—a rare occurrence with the circle. Sometime after the processes outlined in that experiment had terminated and the medium had regained her weight, I carried out an experiment the results of which are to my mind significant and interesting.

The medium being seated on the weighing-machine, her weight + chair + drawing-board balanced at 9 st. 10 lb. 12 oz. I said to the operators, "Please take 2 lb. or thereabouts off the weight of the medium, keep her balanced at that, and rap as loudly as you can." In a very short time after my request her weight was reduced, as evidenced by the steelyard falling against the bottom stop, but I found when I moved the rider back that more than the 2 lb. desired had been removed. I therefore told the operators to add a little to her weight, which they immediately did, but they slightly overstepped the mark, and I had to ask for a trifle to be taken off again. This slight adding and subtracting of weight was done at my request three or four times until the machine just about balanced at the required reduction. It was interesting to see how steadily the operators could hold the reduced weight when once told they had obtained it. Then they rapped. With 2 lb. off (or within a trifle of 2 lb.) the raps were quite soft; and on inquiry if that was the loudest they could do, they answered in the affirmative. Then I asked for more weight to be taken off the medium, about 4 lb. total. The operators overstepped the mark, and I told them, as before, to add on a little weight, when they went a little too far in the other direction. I had to tell them nearly a dozen times to add or subtract a small amount of weight in order to get the rider just to balance at the 4 lb. reduction required. But finally they were successful. Then they rapped, and this time the raps were louder. I asked for a 7 lb. reduction in weight, when the whole process had to be gone over again. When final balance was obtained the raps were very loud. Then again with 10 lb. off, the loudest raps, really blows in this case, were heard. The medium's weight could still be greatly diminished, but I noticed that further reduction seemed to add little or nothing to the intensity of the raps. The extraordinary part of the experiment was the way the operators could, at my request, take off or add on minute amounts of weight, as small as a quarter of a pound or less, in order to make the medium balance at the amount desired, and how they could hold the reduced weight steady once it was obtained.

Experiment 87: A photograph.

I am going to describe now a psychic photograph. It was taken by a friend of mine, under my supervision, on Saturday evening, 23rd Oct. 1915, in my own house. I do not place it in the same category as my other experiments, because I personally am not an expert in photography, and because others had a hand in taking and developing it. Nevertheless, although not up to the standard of test photography, it is an absolutely genuine production. In my articles to *Light* I left the description of this psychic photograph till near the end of the series, because I had hoped to be able to take others and thus corroborate the result obtained. But though I and the circle have gone to great trouble over the matter, we have never been able to duplicate it. Many of my other experiments have been gone over again and again, some as often as a dozen times, and I am prepared at the present moment to carry out any of them with the certainty of success—so long, of course, as the operators and members of the circle are willing. But with this photograph it is different. However as I have already said, it is a perfectly genuine production, as those concerned in it are willing to testify on oath if necessary; and as it has excited so much interest amongst those of my scientific friends who have examined it, I do not consider myself justified in withholding it, more especially as it is in all likelihood the only one of its kind in existence.

Although the print shows the structure to be described below quite clearly, I do not think it would reproduce well, and I will use a diagram for descriptive purposes.

The circle had assembled with the object of obtaining flashlight photographs of the levitated table. During the whole of the day Miss Kathleen Goligher, the principle medium, had been suffering from a cold and a sore throat, and I thought of postponing the séance; but feeling a little better in the evening, she desired that it should be held. The circle sat in its usual order, with the medium at the top end of the room. The camera was placed in position near the bottom end and focussed upon the table. I decided to wait for the photograph until the latter half of the séance. In the meantime we had a display of rapping, levitation, etc. After half an hour or so of this, phenomena ceased, and I told the operators to rap when they were ready for the photograph. During the period of waiting the operators asked us various questions about the height we desired the table to be levitated, the method of procedure with the flashlight, and so on. Then after a time they levitated the table steadily and kept it in the air for several minutes, giving us the impression that they were practising. A further lull followed, and after a time a request from them that, although the table was not levitated, we should try the flashlight, with the object, as it seemed to me, of discovering what would happen to their psychic system of equilibrium when the powerful light should suddenly burst forth. We decided that it would be well to expose a plate during the flash, although we did not expect any result. The circle was widened a little at the bottom end, Master Goligher and Miss Lily Goligher moving a little apart, though keeping their hands joined in the usual way. The flashlight exposure was made (the reader is to remember that the table was not levitated). Then after a little the operators told us they could do no more that evening owing to the condition of the medium. I did not think there was the least likelihood of anything being on the exposed plate, but a surprise was in store when it was developed. The matter is, in my opinion, worthy of being described in detail.

It is obvious this kind of experiment has not the same degree of certainty about it as ordinary tests with weighing apparatus, etc. Further photographs may yet reveal discrepancies in some of my conclusions, and the reader must bear this in mind. Fig. 41 will enable the explanation to be the more easily understood. The following are my analysis and interpretation:—

From about the centre of the left forearm (A) of Master S. Goligher, who is in trance, is seen issuing a vertical column of whitish translucent material about 4 in. in diameter. It comes from his arm at right angles to it, rises about a foot into the air, gradually bending over in the form of an arch (B), and proceeding to (K), which is just on the camera side of the table (standing on the floor in front of the medium), and about a foot above the floor. From (K) a column of about the same or a little greater diameter, and of the same whitish translucent colour, rises vertically into the air, and terminates at (D), at a height of about 5 ft. from the floor. Up to the point (E) the column is of uniform density throughout, and, though thin, has its boundaries well defined. The pattern of the wall-paper is quite easily seen through it. From (E) upwards the column becomes denser and whiter, and at the summit (D) it becomes opaque, so that the wall-paper can no longer be seen through it.

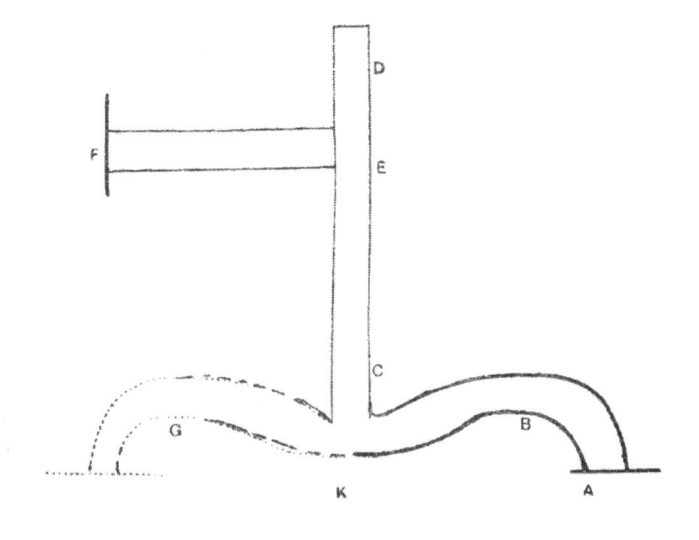

Figure 41

At the top it can be seen to be bending over and backwards, and it descends behind the upward column to the point (E). The opacity at the summit is perhaps due to the eye looking through a double thickness of column, the ascending and descending portions, and to the fact that the psychic stuff has exhausted its velocity at the top. In its descent its boundaries are no longer uniform, but sinuous, and its density not uniform, but patchy. The descending column is easily made out behind the ascending one owing to this patchy appearance and wavy outline. At (E) the descending column branches off horizontally to the left, and enters the top of the chest of the medium (F, Miss Kathleen Goligher).

In the diagram I have drawn a dotted arch (G) from the medium's arm to the point (K) at the bottom of the column. This is not visible owing to the position of the sitters and to the table intervening, but I am assuming it is there. The very bottom part of the column (K) is also not visible owing to an arm of one of the sitters being in the way; but the chances are, from the formation of the arch entering it, that it terminates well above the floor. Also, from the point (E) of the column a very faint outline of about the column's diameter can be made out proceeding in the opposite direction to that of the medium, and presumably entering the chest of Miss Anna Goligher.

It seems to me that we are possibly witnessing in this photograph something of the mechanism of levitation. The most important matter that it hints at is *the circulation of the psychic fluid*. This fluid appears to be sent along the arch to the base of the column, and to be projected vertically upwards to the top, where its kinetic energy becomes exhausted, and then to fall downwards behind the uprising column till on a level with the medium's chest, whence it is drawn, in a horizontal stream, into her body. I have for some time suspected that something like this was the case. If the reader will refer to Experiment 66 he will find in a tabulation there given that after a séance of an hour and a half the medium at the most had only lost two ounces in weight. The whole photograph suggests that the medium is in reality a psychic pump, with a complete pressure system. Perhaps during levitation, the vertical column is under the table, in which case the pressure range would be much greater than is here shown. For in the present example the psychic fluid seems to be losing its energy owing to being projected upwards against its own weight only, much in the way a vertical jet of water does.

On Sunday 31st October 1915, I interrogated the operators with reference to the photograph. They informed me positively and emphatically, by means of raps, that they had purposely set up the whole picture as a means of explaining to me the mechanism of levitation; that the psychic fluid circulates as I have described; and that my description of the processes involved is accurate. In addition they declared that an arch proceeds from each person forming the circle, the one from the medium being by far the strongest and most powerful, and that from the part (E) of the column the return psychic stream does not only proceed to the medium, but that other branches go to each sitter, though, as in the case of the arches, the medium is principally involved. They declared that during levitation the column is under the table, but that the processes I have sketched are still in operation, though on a more intensive scale.

CHAPTER XIII

GENERAL CONCLUSIONS

I have come to the general conclusion from the results of my experimental work, and from observation of the circle extending over two and a half years, that all the phenomena produced are caused by flexible rod-like projections from the body of the medium; that these rods are the prime cause of the phenomena, whether they consist of levitations, movements of the table about the floor, rapping's, touchings, or other variations. The principle characteristics of a rod are as follows:—

(1) It is capable of being pushed straight out from the body of the medium and being pulled straight into the body of the medium. It has not an indefinite limit of extension, but its end can reach, under favourable conditions, to a distance of about 5 feet from her body, and can there act on the table and move it about. Whether the rod gets thinner as it is pushed out from her body I am not able to say, although I should think it likely. The medium's end of the rod, as it is pulled back into her body, is absorbed in her; perhaps the rod is ultimately made up of great bundles of thread-like projections and the whole rod is anchored to her like the roots of a tree.

(2) The rod is capable of to-and-fro motion horizontally over a considerable arc, and can thus move bodies about within the circle formed by the sitters; it has also a limited motion in a vertical plane.

(3) The rod, while capable of in-and-out movement from the medium's body, can be fixed or locked at any required position within is limits of extension, so that in such position it becomes a cantilever.

(4) The rod can transmit pulling and pushing forces.

(5) The free end of the rod is capable (at least sometimes) of gripping bodies by adhesion.

(6) All the motions of the rod are worked from within the body of the medium.

(7) The dimensions of the rod can vary greatly; its cross-section may have different values, and various modifications can be made of the shape and condition of its free end. For ordinary rapping a certain amount of matter seems to be concentrated near the end; and for other forms of rapping, such as the imitation of the bouncing ball, sawing, scraping, etc., it seems as though other modifications and dispositions were made. For levitation a special form of the rod is used, is free end being bent up and gripping the table by adhesion underneath. Nevertheless, whether for levitation, rapping, or other phenomena, a rod-like projection is always used, though this projection may assume special forms and shapes, and have different degrees of flexibility and stiffness to suit the production of different phenomena.

In the light of this theory a large amount of the physical phenomena of the séance room become somewhat more intelligible. Take as an example "direct voice" phenomena, where a metal trumpet some 3 or 4 ft. long is carried round the room in the air for many minutes at a time, while voices purport to speak through it to the sitters. It is possible, and even probable, that the trumpet is gripped adhesively by the free end of a rod-projection from the medium, and is carried about on the end of this rod, all kinds of motion being possible, as explained above.

Having arrived at the rod-projection theory, it becomes necessary to endeavour to find out a little about the composition of the rod, in what manner it possesses the characteristics of a solid body, and so on; and I wish to state here that I have no satisfactory theory to offer. In the few remarks I am going to make I will endeavour to summarise some of the facts I have observed, and state a few of the deductions from such facts, so that at a later date they may be co-ordinated with the results of further experimental work, and help, I hope, in the final solution of the problem.

The first thing I wish to mention in this connection is that occasionally during levitation I have felt immediately below the under surface of the table (not near the floor) something that appears to be matter. It has a cold, clammy, reptilian feeling, impossible adequately to describe in words, but which, once felt, the experimenter always recognises again. I was struck, when reading over some of Dr. Schrenck-Notzing's experiments on materialisation, to notice that in the first stages of materialisation the matter issuing from the medium gave the same or a very similar sensation to the hand; the feeling being described as cold and clammy, one of the assistants even remarking that it felt as though a small reptile were lying on his hand. There is therefore little doubt in my mind that the stuff issuing from the medium in the first stages of materialisation and the stuff under the top of the levitated table are essentially one and the same. The stuff coming from Dr. Schrenck-Notzing's medium was observed issuing sometimes from her mouth, and was perfectly visible, while any such matter under the table is not visible. It must therefore, if essentially the same, be of a more rudimentary quality, a stage further back than that made use of for materialisation. The matter under the table felt quite still and at rest, and, in fact, when I moved my hand to and fro amongst it, the table soon dropped, showing that it was essential to levitation. Indeed, the operators were always very chary about letting me work in amongst it, the only thing in that connection they did not object to greatly being the moving of a *thin* rod across the space occupied by it.

In addition to the under surface of the levitated table, I have *often* felt this same quality of matter, with its same cold, clammy, reptile-like feel, near the ankles of the medium when rapping was taking place close to her feet at the commencement of a séance. For an important séance I have never placed my hand near the place from which this stuff was issuing; for I soon found by experience in early trials that if I did so the rapping was stopped for quite a long time, and could seemingly only be restarted with difficulty. During impromptu circles, however, or because of ignorance at the commencement of my experiments, I have often interrupted the flow of this matter, with the inevitable result of temporarily stopping phenomena. The main point, however, is that near the medium, indeed quite close to her body, the same quality of matter is present during rapping phenomena as is present under the levitated table; and not only so, but in the former case *it is in motion* in the direction *from body of medium outwards*, as can easily be observed by the spore-like sensation as of soft particles moving gently against the hand. During levitation of the table I have never actually interrupted the line of stress from medium to table with my hand but I have placed a delicate pressure-recording apparatus in that line (see Experiments 59 and 60), with the result that it was shown there was a mechanical pressure close to the body of the medium (although the conditions of the experiment allow of its being a pressure of very small magnitude) acting outwards from her to the levitated table; and furthermore, the placing of the apparatus in the stress-line caused the table to drop. Also the place of origin of this stress-line in the body of the medium appeared to be near the lower part of the trunk. It seems likely, therefore, that the pressure against the testing apparatus was due to a flow of particles of the same kind of matter as can be felt under the levitated table and such as issues from the ankles of the medium during rapping near her feet. It remains to be added that the operators were annoyed at my inference with the line medium to table, and told me so by vigorous raps. There can be little doubt this is the vital part of the mechanism of levitation, and it is the part that cannot be interfered with if we desire phenomena.

My proposition, then, is this:— An essential part of the levitating cantilever (or modified rod-projection) consists of particles of cold, clammy, disagreeable matter which in the end of the cantilever near the medium (the fixed end) are in motion outwards from her, and which under the table are at rest. Also, for the construction of the rapping rods the same kind of matter is necessary; and it likewise, in the end attached to the medium, is moving outwards from her.

I next wish to call attention to what happens at levitation. I have shown during the course of my experiments that it seems as though the preliminary process to actual levitation is the laying of some kind of a loose link from medium to table, or, if a compression balance is under the table, from medium to pan of the balance. Let us suppose that this loose link consists of some fine threads of matter similar to the organic matter that issues from the mouth of Dr. Schrenck-Notzing's medium, only much finer and beyond the reach of visibility. Dr. Schrenck-Notzing has shown that the thready stuff from his medium can twist and squirm and move about and make purposeful motions as though it were alive and conscious. The levitating threads may also be supposed to find their way by similar movements from the body of the medium to the under surface of the table, and thus to found a foundation for the levitating structure to be immediately erected. For what happens for half a minute after the preliminary arrangements are complete? The levitating force is the applied, and grows at a fairly uniform rate until levitation occurs, the growth of the force taking from five to six seconds. It seems as though the essential threads, or bundle of threads, being in position, a force is exerted along their axis which stiffens them and makes the bundle into a solid rod.

There are other observations which show that the levitating cantilever consists of a very fine (possibly organic) thread-like structure which is stiffened and made rigid by some kind of force being applied along it, rather than of a system of rays or anything of that nature. One of these is that the structure can transmit both pushing and pulling forces of large magnitude. I cannot imagine any system of stresses, unless they had a physical basis, being able to do this with conditions such as they are in the séance room. Then again the change of direction of the free end of the cantilever as it rises in columnar form beneath the table would seem also to presuppose some kind of interconnected physical structure, perhaps of a cobwebby form, which is filled out and made stiff by its interstices being under some kind of pressure. The fact that the levitating force grows from the instant of application at a fairly slow and uniform rate, and is not applied instantly, would indicate that the force exerted along the structure, whatever its nature, has the function of stiffening it. So that, taking everything into consideration, my basic idea of the rod-projection is this:— It consists fundamentally of a bundle of very fine threads thrust out from the body of the medium, which are practically transparent and hence invisible; the threads being intimately connected and touching and adhering to one another. These threads, in the manner of those observed during Dr. Schrenck-Notzing's experiments on materialisation, can move and twist about by forces applied to them from within the body of the medium (possibly they are directly connected to the nervous system of the medium by nerve filaments or in some other way); the threads are gradually projected to the space beneath the table, and their free ends are attached to its under surface. When this has been attained, a force is applied along their axis, gradually and uniformly, with the result that the system of threads (or cable, it would perhaps be well to call it) is gradually stiffened and becomes a rigid girder projecting from the medium and able to levitate the table. That a preliminary thread-like structure, which is afterward stiffened, is first sent out from the medium is also likely from the following experimental result:— When the séance table had the two light cross-bars near the bottom of the legs removed (see Experiment 52), the operators seemed to have some small difficulty for a little time afterwards in levitating the table as completely and easily as before. They seemed to have to make new adjustments, as it were, and to get used to making these adjustments. I think the preliminary thread-like structure from the medium took hold of these cross-bars in the process of shaping the cantilever—i.e. they were used as vantage-points from which to erect the structure. However, it wasn't long before levitation without them was as strong and powerful as ever; some new arrangement having undoubtedly been devised by the operators.

The question then arises: What sort of force is it that is applied along the axis of the threads or fibres? Is it some mysterious, totally unknown force of which we have not the faintest conception, or is it a force with whose laws we are acquainted? The only answer I can give is that I do not know. It may turn out eventually to be a very simple matter.

I wish to state here what a clairvoyante saw at the circle—a clairvoyante who has many claims to recognition,—as she described it to me. She says that under the table, close to the under surface and extending down for a little way, she saw a whitish vapoury substance, somewhat like smoke, and when the table was levitated this substance seemed to increase in density, i.e. in whiteness. When a visitor to the circle sat on the table, in order that it should tilt and throw him off, she saw this substance below the table get very white and dense just previous to the movement which actually tilted the table. So much so, in fact, was she able to see the variation in the density and whiteness of the substance, and its relation to the magnitude of the force applied, that she was able to call out that a movement was about to occur before it actually occurred, by noticing the density and opacity increasing. She says that this whitish substance was only to be seen under the top of the table, and *did not reach the floor.* Also a great band of it came from the left side of the medium with a kind of rotary motion, and was continuous with that under the table. From *all* the other sitters a very thin band, like a ribbon, also came and was continuous with the mass under the table. Nowhere did any of these bands, the comparatively huge one from the medium, or the thin and paltry ones from the sitters, touch the floor. The clairvoyante says she also saw various spirit forms and spirit hands manipulating the psychic stuff, but we may leave that out of consideration and confine our attention to what is mentioned above.

The remarkable fact is plain that the clairvoyante's description tallies in an extraordinary way with my deductions from the experiments. In the first place, she says there was none of the white filmy stuff on or near the floor beneath the levitated table. Experiments have absolutely convinced me that there is no psychic pressure on the floor or on the platform placed less than 3 in. above the floor, and that the psychic reaction gradually increases with the height of the platform. In the second place, she says the different degrees of apparent density of the substance enabled her roughly to gauge the magnitude of the psychic force. Now, it is absolutely certain that the pressure below the table in the act of levitation is applied gradually, and only reaches a maximum after five or six seconds, which gave me time to call out that a levitation was about to occur, well before it did actually occur. In the third place, the great bulk of the whitish substance was seen proceeding from the medium, but there was also a thin band from each sitter. Now, experiment shows that when the table is levitated, about 97 per cent of the reaction is upon the medium; that on one of the other sitters there is also a small but nevertheless perceptible reaction. The coincidence, to say the least of it, is thought-provoking. The clairvoyante says she saw the whitish substance issuing from the *left* side of the medium. As a matter of fact, the medium, during the course of her development, has occasionally been troubled with a soreness in her left side, which may not unreasonably be supposed to be due to the large quantity of psychic stuff which may issue thence during levitation.

If we may take the vision of the clairvoyante as accurate, it would appear that a whitish substance is present under the top part of the levitated table, the whiteness or density increasing with the magnitude of the psychic force applied. This substance is not visible to normal vision, for often I have looked right below levitated tables from one side of the circle to the other, and have seen nothing. Nevertheless, for all that, as already mentioned, something in the nature of a cold clammy substance appears to be there. Therefore it is probably this substance that the clairvoyante, with her abnormal perception, really saw. In this connection it is well to remember that the photograph (Experiment 87) shows a white, filmy, translucent substance, apparently projected from the body of one of the sitters, and that this substance also has different degrees of density. Possibly the stuff shown in the photograph, the stuff the clairvoyante saw, and the stuff I felt under the table and near the ankles of the medium are one and the same. At any rate, if the clairvoyante really saw this stuff, it is reasonable to believe that the different degrees of density she observed in it are really varying degrees of density of the stuff itself; that is to say, that the magnitude of the applied psychic force is somewhat directly proportional to the density of the matter taken from the medium. From which we arrive at the inference:— the magnitude of the psychic force is directly proportional to the density of the matter in the stress line from medium to table.

The stiffness of the levitating cantilever would then be more or less proportional to the density of the matter packed into or among the threads or fibres issuing from the medium.

That some kind of a thread-like base or substratum is based as a foundation for the phenomena at the circle is also inferentially deduced from the following, which, however, I have not personally observed. Mr. Morrison, whose place in the circle is on the right-hand side of the medium, and who holds her right hand throughout the séance (except on special occasions when hands are on knees), and who has been sitting once a week on an average for a period of over three years, informs me that occasionally, when psychic energy has been weak, he has felt a loose kind of flabby projection striking him on the knee or other part of the body. It is reasonable to suppose that this is a rapping rod which the operators have been unable to make rigid through lack of psychic energy. Mr. Morrison being the director of the circle, the operators often gently touch him when they desire to attract his attention to something that is hindering phenomena; usually their touch is quite firm, but on a few occasions, as mentioned, he has felt the loose, baggy projection flapping against him.

The effect of light is generally speaking, so well known on the production of physical phenomena, that I do not intend to say much about it. The obvious fact is that the less light the more intense the phenomena. I have come to the conclusion that light affects the rigidity of the rapping rods, i.e. the rods cannot be made stiff if strong light is plating on them. As a case in point, I would refer the reader to p. 68, where it is shown that with too much light, or with badly regulated light, the raps were not sharp and distinct as they should be, but were soft and dull as though the end of the rod itself were soft; in other words, the rigidity of the rods were affected. I do not think that the light affects the substratum fibres so much as the matter that is packed into them to stiffen them (if there is anything in the fibre theory); i.e. I think that the cold clammy matter above mentioned cannot exist in the presence of strong light. Possibly it is of complicated chemical structure, belonging to the nervous elements of the body, and the action of light causes molecular breakdown. There is the more reason to suppose that something like this takes place inasmuch as it is found by experience that light of long wave-length, i.e. red light, is least deleterious.

Of course in the séance room the factors of reflection, refraction, and absorption of the light used have to be taken into consideration. In this regard I will mention a rather curious case which occurred at one of my séances. As already mentioned, I used at my experimental circles an ordinary flame gas-jet enclosed in a metal lantern, two sides of the lantern being replaced by rectangular pieces of red glass which could slide up and down in grooves. The intensity of the red light thus produced could be considerably varied by means of an ordinary gas tap. For most of the séances this lamp was fixed to the mantelpiece; for a late séance it was taken from the mantelpiece and fixed a foot higher up the wall, with the idea of leaving the floor a little more in shadow and of giving greater luminosity in the higher parts of the room. The séance commenced, but, as after twenty minutes or so very little seemed to be doing—a most unusual occurrence,—I began to wonder what was the matter. Shortly afterwards, by means of raps, the operators spelt out the following:—

"Could you place the lamp lower down?"

After a lot of trouble, we succeeded in fixing the lamp in its original position on the mantelpiece, when phenomena of great intensity commenced. I could see practically no difference in the degree of visibility for the two positions. I think, however, that in its higher position light was being reflected from the whitewashed roof to the floor, and this is a matter psychic investigators should bear in mind. I have noticed, also, that the operators find difficulty in applying psychic force to polished bodies, and that they prefer a rough, darkish surface. But this, of course, may have nothing to do with the light, and may be due to the fact that the adhesive qualities of the rod-projection are best suited to rough surfaces.

The question is often asked: Why do you not apply to the operators themselves for the solution of the problems relating to the phenomena? In fact this question was raised during the running of my series of articles in *Light*, and is a perfectly legitimate one. Moreover, I was interested in it during the course of all my work, and always had it in mind; indeed, the reader of this book will find that here and there I have asked questions of the operators as to modes of procedure, as to how things were done, and so on, and that I have either acted on the suggestions given or have examined any of the statements made.

In the first place, the operators themselves do not seem to know much about the scientific aspect of the phenomena they produce. If I may hazard an opinion, I would say that they are only aware of the broad outlines of what they are doing, just as we are, for instance, when we send an electric current along a wire. At any rate, I am convinced that the operators know next to nothing of force magnitudes and reactions. Their idea as to the prime cause of the phenomena is "power." For instance, when I inquired how a certain reaction effect was obtained, they spelt out by raps the word "power." That is to say, they have no exact scientific knowledge of details. They are like the workman who knows by experience what depth of cut to take on a job in the lathe, at what speed to run the machine, etc., but who has little idea of the cutting force exerted by the edge of the tool, or of the exact horse-power necessary to drive the machine. Nevertheless, as might be supposed, if some small material thing is interfering with their results they are quick enough to rap out a request that it be rectified, just as a workman would know to sharpen his tool if its cutting quality was defective. Thus on one occasion they asked that a piece of cloth should be placed on the drawing-board, on another that the light should be placed nearer the floor, and on another that one of the sitters should alter position. Small things like these, which interfere with the intensity of their phenomena, they seem to understand; but as to what form of energy it is they utilise to lift the table or cause the rap they seem to know little.

What I have said above refers to communications received by raps when Miss Goligher was perfectly normal, as she always is at all experimental circles. Occasionally, however, when I have desired it, she has gone into trance, not for physical phenomena, but to allow me to talk to the entities purporting to speak through her. One of these, who says he was a medical man while on earth, and whose function at the circle is to look after the health of the medium during phenomena, has told me (a little obscurely, it is true) that there are two kinds of substance taken from the members of the circle and used in the production of phenomena. One of these is taken in comparatively large quantities from medium and sitters, and is all, or nearly all, returned to them at the close of the séance. The other is taken in minute quantities, and can only be obtained from the medium, and this stuff cannot be returned to her because when it is used for phenomenal purposes its structure is broken up. It consists of the most vital material in the mediums body—stuff from the interior of her nerve cells,—and only the most minute quantity can be removed without injury to the medium. I give his statement, of course, only as a matter of interest.

One other point. The operators are always strongly affirmative, strongly negative, or strongly doubtful in replies to questions. I have never known them say they could do something and then fail to do it; likewise if they say they cannot do a thing, it will not be done; if they mention the matter as doubtful, they try to accomplish it, usually successfully. So also, in answer to questions with regard to the production of the phenomena, I have always found them eager to tell me anything they can; and if they affirm any one of my theories is right, wrong, or doubtful, I have always found, by deduction from the experiments themselves, or by later experiments, that it was as they said. I have never known them volunteer information (with the exception of the case of the "doctor" referred to above), but they are always willing strongly to affirm or strongly to deny the general sense of my conclusions. In addition, I have sometimes thought they have brought to my attention in roundabout ways phases of an experiment I should have otherwise overlooked.

Besides the main processes resulting in levitation, rapping etc., there are various preliminary operations taking place at the circle which I have not studied in any very definite way, but which, nevertheless, are of great interest. I will conclude by saying a few words about them.

For the first half-hour or so after the opening of the séance I have found it advisable that the members of the circle should clasp hands in chain order, i.e. the hands of each person should be held by the hands of the persons on either side of him. After the expiration of that time it is *usually* immaterial whether hands are kept clasped, or whether each sitter places his hands on his knees. I say this is usually the case, but it is not always so. It is only true when the séance has been a good one, with phenomena occurring plentifully. If phenomena have been weak, the clasping of hands and the placing of them on the knees is usually fatal to further manifestations unless the chain order is resumed.

All this points to the fact that at a normally good séance the sitting, generally speaking, may be divided into two parts—a part which is more or less unstable, where the operators are chiefly engaged in preparatory work, and a part where psychic affairs have reached a state of equilibrium. I have often watched the two processes—the stage of preliminary operations and the stage of balance.

To my mind, the two processes suggest physical analogies which are helpful. Let us think of a large tank situated well above the ground level, which has to be filled with water from the ground by means of several varieties of steam pumps. The sitters may be likened to the steam pumps, and their various psychic capacities and conditions may be considered to resemble various classes and designs in the pumps. The filling of the water tank is equivalent to producing a region of psychic pressure in the neighbourhood of the medium. I find that the psychic tank takes about half an hour to fill at the Goligher circle. Very seldom is it completely filled; when it is, there results a wonderful phenomenal sitting. At séances where the accumulated amount of psychic energy is small—where the tank is only a quarter filled, say—the psychic pumps have to be kept more or less continually going. The spasmodic jerking seen in the bodies of the sitters is in effect the visible working of the psychic pumps.

Let us suppose that the séance is a good one, and that it is possible for the members of the circle to place hands on knees and thus become physically isolated from one another. In that case the stage of psychic equilibrium has been reached—the psychic tank has been filled,—and a reservoir of psychic energy has been accumulated in the neighbourhood of the medium, from which the operators can draw to produce phenomena. Now, what kind of potential energy is it? Is it chemical, pressure, electrical, heat energy, or indeed some form quite unknown to us? Personally—and now the reader must remember I am again in the region of hypothesis, though of hypothesis derived from a considerable amount of observation—I am inclined to think it is a form of chemical energy associated with the human nervous system. The opportunities for research here are unlimited. At any rate, I think there can be little doubt that this psychic energy is associated with particles of matter. For instance, a cold wind is often apparent at the commencement of a séance—a cold wind which often disappears after a time. I think it probable that this cold effect is due to material evaporation from the bodies of the sitters; not to a large or even appreciable amount of evaporation, but nevertheless to the evaporation of definite particles of matter. The reservoir of psychic energy accumulated presumably near the medium does not appreciably affect her weight. I have weighed her before the séance, and then again when the séance has been in operation for an hour or so, with psychic equilibrium well established, but *I found no appreciable difference in the two results.* In fact it would appear that the accumulated psychic energy is only associated with a small and perhaps an inappreciable amount of matter. For all that, of course, it may have considerable magnitude.

In order that we may form some kind of mental picture of what occurs to medium and sitters, I offer the following hypothesis. It is very imperfect, but may be useful in the meantime in default of anything better:—

Sitters clasp hands. Spasmodic jerking occurs. A cold wind is sometimes felt in the wrists and hands. After half an hour or so the jerking ceases or becomes less pronounced.

Interpretation: Operators are acting on the brains of the sitters and thence on their nervous systems. Small particles, it may even be molecules, are driven off the nervous system, out through the bodies of sitters at wrists, hands, fingers, or elsewhere. These small particles, now free, have a considerable amount of latent energy inherent in them, an energy which can react on any human nervous system with which they come into contact. This system of energised particles flows round the circle, probably partly through the bodies of the sitters, and probably partly on the periphery of their bodies. The stream, by gradual augmentation from the sitters, reaches the medium at a high degree of "tension," energises her, receives increment from her, traverses the circle again, and so on. Finally when the tension is sufficiently great, the circulating process ceases, and the energised particles collect on or are attached to the nervous system of the medium, who has henceforth a reservoir from which to draw. The operators having now a good supply of the right kind of energy at their disposal, viz. nerve energy, can act upon the body of the medium, who is so constituted that gross matter from her body can, by means of the nervous system applied to it, be actually temporarily detached from its usual position and projected into the séance room.

LIST OF EXPERIMENTS

Experiment Number	Subject	Page
1	Phonograph records of Raps	20
2	Reaction on medium	29
3	Reaction on medium	30
4	Reaction on medium	31
5	Reaction on sitter	34
6	Reaction on sitter	34
7	Reaction on medium	36
8	Reaction on medium	36
9	Reaction on medium	37
10	Table moving along floor	37
11	Various movements of table	38
12	Observation of weighing-machine	39
13	Table tilted on two legs	39
14	Table pulled towards medium	40
15	Table pushed from medium	40
16	Calculation of levitating pressure	44
17	Calculation of levitating pressure	45
18	Muscular force on table	46
19	Two resistances for table	48
20	Unyielding resistance for table	49
21	Overturning of table	50
22	Increased and decreased weight of table	51
23	Table levitated upside down	51
24	Muscular force on upturned table	51
25	Experimenter sitting on table	52
26	Maximum psychic force on table	52
27	Unsymmetrical loading of table	53
28	Ringing an electric bell	54
29	Trumpet pulled	56
30	Table pulled from edge of circle	56
31	Handkerchief on floor	57
32	Light placed on table	59
33	Sliding body under table	60
34	Exploring region below legs of table	62
35	Exploring region under table	62
36	Glass tube below table	64
37	Manometer below table	64

LIST OF EXPERIMENTS

Experiment Number	Subject	Page
38	Reaction on floor	66
39	Ringing electric bell	68
40	Levitation above weighing-machine	70
41	Levitation above weighing-machine	72
42	Levitation above weighing-machine	74
43	Levitation above weighing-machine	75
44	Compression balance below table	79
45	Compression balance below table	82
46	Table tilting above balance	84
47	Compression balance tests	85
48	Horizontal component of reaction	86
49	Horizontal component of reaction	87
50	Vertical downward reaction	88
51	Reaction and height of platform	91
52	Reaction and height of platform	94
53	Stool levitated above balance	96
54	Electrical test for reaction	98
55	Reaction on medium	100
56	Crackling sound in table	101
57	Thud under table	101
58	Electroscope under table	102
59	Space between medium and table	102
60	Space between medium and table	103
61	Reaction on floor	104
62	Condition of medium	104
63	Weight of levitating structure	105
64	Preparation for levitation	105
65	Actual matter below table	107
66	Weight loss by sitters	108
67	Fluorescence	110
68	Psychic pull	121
69	Psychic pull	124
70	Trumpet movements	129
71	Medium's weight and raps	133
72	Medium's weight and raps	135
73	Medium and commencement of séance	136
74	Distinction between levitation and rapping	139
75	Bombardment during rapping	140
76	Shape of rap	141

Experiment Number	Subject	Page
77	Typewriter test	147
78	Raps on putty	148
79	Electroscope below table	152
80	Psychic touching of electroscope	153
81	Psychic touching of electroscope	153
82	Psychic touching of electroscope	154
83	Electric shock test	155
84	Phosphorescence	155
85	Fluorescence	156
86	Delicacy of actions on medium	156
87	Psychic photograph	158

SDU PUBLICATIONS

SDU Publications' aim is to publish books by or about some of the outstanding mediums who demonstrated their abilities from 1848 to the current day, and thereby keep their names alive.

Mediums we have re-published books by or about:
  Daniel Dunglas Home
  Emma Hardinge
  Estelle Roberts
  Helen Hughes
  J.J. Morse
  Margery Crandon
  Nettie Colburn Maynard

For details or to request our current catalogue:
  Tel: 01909 489828
  Email: ....mail@s-upton.com
  Website: ....www.sdu3.com or